So You Want To Be President...

How To Get Elected On Your Campus

Edited By

Butch Oxendine

Oxendine PUBLISHING

P.O. Box 14081, Gainesville, FL 32604-2081

Published by Oxendine Publishing, Inc.,
P.O. Box 14081, Gainesville, FL 32604-2081.

First Printing, August 1997.
Copyright © 1997 by Oxendine Publishing, Inc.
All rights reserved.

Special Thanks

The entire staff at Oxendine Publishing contributed to this book:

☛ Managing Editor Kay Quinn and Assistant Editor Teresa Beard edited and proofed. I'm sure they feel like they know all of these presidents intimately by now. Interns Patti Ashley, Tara Dolan, and Sara Lyle also helped proofread. Iris Schubert helped with research.

☛ Art Director Jeff Riemersma designed the book, handled typesetting, and scanned the art and photos—and put up with numerous "final" changes.

☛ Business Manager Diane Eskridge processed orders and handled billing customers. Val Grodewald helped with shipping orders and correspondence. Tammy Beard helped prepare mailings.

I'm also grateful for input from the subscribers of several listservers around the country. Most of the contributors in this book came *directly* from suggestions offered by listserver subscribers. Thank you!

And lastly, I thank each of the contributors. All of them devoted hours of work to this project, and their efforts show!

We're excited to produce the second in a series of helpful books for campus leaders nationwide, by expanding on articles that we publish in *Student Leader*, *Florida Leader*, and *Careers & Majors*. We have three other books in progress and hope to publish them by the end of the year.

I also thank my wife Kathy for her encouragement and support of this project.

Table of Contents

Table of Contents

Forward

Many Student Government elections mimic those of local, statewide, or even national campaigns. There's often just as much or more mudslinging, negative campaigning, and infighting among "power groups" and political parties.

With some SG budgets ballooning to as high as $7 million annually and other schools offering five-figure salaries to SG leaders, it's no wonder that many students vie for the top spots around the country.

Being a campus power broker can yield many personal perks, such as access to dignitaries who visit campus and networking chances for future job prospects. SG leaders often gain many other skills: management, communications, public relations, and budgeting that benefit them in whatever career field they choose.

Student Government elections have become big business. Running for office sometimes costs thousands of dollars and involves hundreds of volunteers giving countless hours.

At some huge institutions such as the University of Florida, the University of Michigan, and Texas A&M University, Student Government elections attract tremendous media attention in and outside of the campus community. Some would argue, probably accurately, that elections at these schools are more closely scrutinized events than even local city council or county commission races.

At many schools — particularly smaller colleges, community colleges, and commuter schools — you still can run and win a campaign on your good name. Just by putting up a few colorful campaign flyers and prodding your friends to head to the polls, you can eke out a victory. But at most colleges and universities, getting elected takes a lot more work.

It's gotten to the point that to have a solid chance to be elected, you need a sophisticated plan complete with fundraising, public relations, and media strategies.

If you're thinking about running for president or another campus leadership position, instead of hiring a high-priced consultant (yeah, right), just read this book. You'll get insight on how these 25 top current and former Student Government officials won their elections. They tell you, in their own words, why they ran for office in the first place, how they chose their platform issues, how they spread the word about their candidacies, and what made them electable. If you have questions, they're even willing to talk with you, and we've provided phone numbers and addresses where you can contact them.

Naturally, not all of the examples will be appropriate for your school, but we've purposely chosen SG leaders from all types of institutions: from large to small enrollments, from men's and women's colleges, and from public and private schools. We've also included community college leaders, non-traditional-aged officers, minorities, and women. There are unopposed candidates and even two-term presidents— the whole gamut. There's bound to be an example or two that you can take to heart and learn from to help you get elected.

Remember, just wanting to be president isn't enough. Assuming that you hope to actually accomplish realistic goals while in office, your motivation must be deeper than padding your own resume. You must have, as Oscar De La Torre writes in his essay, "an innate desire to help your fellow students."

It's wrong to run so that you can get free tickets to events and games, meet dignitaries and celebrities who come to campus, and get dates because you're the big cheese on campus. But if you run for office because you care about helping students solve problems and making their college experience better, then you can win and feel proud that you're giving something back to the college or university that you love.

W.H. "Butch" Oxendine, Jr.,
Editor

The Editor's Winning Strategy At Lake City Community College & The University of Florida

By Butch Oxendine
1982-83 Student Government Association vice president
Lake City Community College, Florida

When I ran for vice president of the Student Government Association at Lake City Community College, my entire campaign strategy was to plaster the campus with flyers saying "Vote for Butch." That was it.

I didn't have an agenda, a platform of ideas, or goals for our administration. I just wanted to be vice president, frankly — it was more of a personal goal at that time than a desire to serve the student body. For a guy who was painfully shy in high school, risking failure in a campuswide election was a major step in helping me gain self-confidence.

On a small rural campus with about 2,000 students, I didn't have to be sophisticated to win. I relied on my name recognition as editor of the campus newspaper, *The Timberchatter*. I would have run for SGA president if I hadn't been editor, but clearly it would be a major conflict of interest to hold high offices in LCCC's two main campus organizations.

When I decided to run, I already was serving as an SGA senator, which naturally helped me attract votes from fellow SGA members. I also got support from the dorms — LCCC is the only community college in the state with campus housing. As a dorm resident and a resident assistant, most of the dorm students (about 150 total) knew me, which helped.

We didn't have candidate debates or any real campaigning, nor did we have a spending limit. I probably spent less than $10 on copies and then put them up myself all around campus on bulletin boards inside buildings. I served as my own campaign manager and staff — none of the candidates needed volunteers.

I won with about 70 percent of the 250 students' votes. Most of my votes came from friends and acquaintances. The single polling booth on campus was in the cafeteria where all of the dorm students came to eat. No doubt this helped me. My opponent was an "outsider" who wasn't well-known on campus, and he didn't live and hang out with the on-campus residents like I did.

Winning my election at LCCC really was a low-key affair compared to the costly campaigns I was involved with later.

A Rude Awakening at the University of Florida

When I transferred to UF, I expected to leap right into campus politics and make an immediate impact, like I had done at LCCC. Little did I know that elections are much more complex, more competitive, more expensive — more everything — than what I was used to.

During the first semester, I "slated" with the "Beach Party" as a senate candidate from one of the off-campus districts. The party had about 40 senate candidates, each of whom chipped in $50 toward our "party" expenses.

I naively assumed that if I walked around my neighborhood, knocked on doors and met my "constituents," I would win handily. I couldn't have been more mistaken.

Our entire party was defeated soundly by hand-picked candidates representing the Greek "power blocks" — fraternities, sororities, and the leadership honorary Blue Key. These blocks strongly "encouraged" their brothers and sisters to first go to the polls, then vote as a block, to ensure that their candidates won. With election turnout typically at about 10 percent of the 35,000 enrollment, Greeks controlled Student Government elections — about 16 percent of all UF students are Greek, and most of them vote. So normally, there was no way for an independent outsider to win in the general election.

I remember sitting in the Orange & Brew, the student hangout where candidates traditionally await election results. I was actually surprised when the voting totals were announced and my name wasn't among the winners. This eye-opening experience turned me off to SG for a time, but I also was starting my publishing "empire" then and had my hands full trying to stay in business, to say the least.

It wasn't until a friend announced his candidacy for student body president nearly two years later that I got involved again. This candidate, while Greek, pitched himself as an SG outsider, battling the "corruption" of Blue Key, which many average students perceived as elitist. He hardly was an outsider, though, as he had been deeply involved in SG before, serving as Traffic Court Chief Justice.

At first, I just helped him design the party's ads for the campus newspaper, *The Independent Florida Alligator*. But I quickly became much more involved, helping write his speeches, sitting in on late-night strategy sessions, and even stooping so low as to spy on *The Alligator*'s printer to find out if the paper planned to endorse our man (we found out it did).

We badgered the big-shot Gator football quarterback into accepting a spot as a senate candidate. Then we included photos of him with our candidates in their cute, bright yellow Beach Party T-shirts. Everything in the campaign was yellow, including newspaper ads, brochures, signs, T-shirts, and buttons, which definitely stood out around campus.

We ran newspaper ads that each cost hundreds of dollars a pop, scheduled radio spots on two popular commercial rock stations, and even debated on local cable TV. We made thousands of copies of platforms and stationed campaign volunteers across campus to pester pedestrians into taking our leaflets and voting Beach.

Amazingly, we spent more than $10,000 getting our candidate elected—and this was in 1985. This money was raised by mandatory donations from the slate of senate candidates and big infusions from the candidate's family. The amount we spent on this campaign was nearly as much as the entire SGA budget when I was at Lake City Community College.

This combination of money, manpower, and marketing worked. Our man came out ahead in the primary election when there were several candidates vying for the top spots, then he won easily in the run-off election. Hundreds of students danced and partied the night away at the Alpha Gamma Rho fraternity house across from campus after learning of our victory.

Two Distinctly Different Types of Campaigns

The differences in these two campaigns are striking — one, with organized, intricate political maneuvering and big expenses; the other, with a low-key, relaxed atmosphere with almost no expenditures or formal campaigning.

But each had its strategies that worked and those that didn't. That's why we've included the experiences of all different types of students and schools — to give you tips and ideas that you may be able to tailor to your own situation and campaign. Good luck!

The Only Two-Time Student Body President in USF History

By David "DQ" Quilleon
1994-96 Student Government President
University of South Florida, Tampa

Introduction

Mr. Quilleon, 25, served two full years as student body president, from April 1994 to May 1996. He was the first candidate to ever win consecutive terms, and also was the first mass communications major to hold the top office. He now is Florida colleges program manager for Best Buddies, an international service organization.

At USF, Quilleon served as Homecoming Director, vice president of the Florida Student Association, and a founding father of Beta Theta Pi Fraternity. He was named 1995 Homecoming King, 1994 Outstanding Greek Male, president of the State Council of Student Body Presidents, and was a member of the University Disciplinary Board.

Here's How DQ Won Back-to-Back Elections At USF

Winning an election isn't an easy task— your campaign must be undertaken with determination and total commitment to victory. Winning a campaign takes time, money, and creativity. You also have to recruit volunteers who are supportive and willing to give of their time and talents. Every rule of the election process must be followed by everyone working on your campaign. You also have to be willing to make personal contact with your constituents.

At the University of South Florida, the 15th largest school in the nation, Student Government campaigns require diligence and a serious commitment. With a diverse population of 36,000 students, including many commuters and non-traditional students, I felt like I need to address the needs of those constituents. Fortunately, I had been working at the main information desk in the Student Union for two years prior to my elections, so I got to hear many complaints and problems that students were having. While it wasn't a formal poll of student opinion, I felt like I had a handle on what issues were bugging students. They had complained to me when I wasn't running for office, so their comments probably were more truthful than had they responded to a survey.

Two of the top issues at USF are the lack of campus parking and the lack of a football team. Campus unity was just about nonexistent, with the exception of the Greek organizations and a few special-interest groups. My campaign focused on acting on these issues.

Word of mouth advertising is best. I also believe that the best type of advertising for your campaign is word of mouth. Everywhere I went, I was marketing my skills and strengths to others, and trying to encourage their friends to endorse me. The personal approach is the ultimate campaign tool. A handshake, eye to eye contact, and a personal conversation about individual concerns are what really influence voters. The size of your school is immaterial. A flyer may bring recognition to you, but you'll get votes and students' loyalty with personal attention.

I tried to appeal to the special-interest groups, even those that I knew probably wouldn't support me, like organizations that my opponents belonged to. I knew I would need the support of the Greeks, as well as leadership groups such as the Ambassadors and the Campus Activities Board. I also focused on appealing to the few thousand students living on campus. The residence halls won't just let you come in and speak anytime, so I recruited friends living there to invite me so that I could walk around the halls and meet students.

Get students motivated to vote. Most students felt detached, so I had to convince them to vote, and then vote for me. Student Government had been besieged by less than ethical budgetary

The University of South Florida's Alisa Cooney and David Quilleon celebrate their election victory at the Marshall Center.

practices and I told them my plan was to bring honor back to SG.

The election I won in April 1994 was the second time I had sought the student body presidency. I first ran just after our Student Government had been shut down in October 1993 because of financial problems and I won the election by 100 votes. But since none of the candidates had earned 50 percent of the vote, there was a run-off, which I lost by a mere 15 votes. I later learned that I had won six of the nine Colleges, but that my defeat probably was the result of a huge turnout at the College of Engineering. My opponents had plastered photos of the vice presidential candidate around the building, and she had stood out front all day encouraging her fellow engineering students to vote — and it worked. Their voting location was very accessible to Engineering students, whereas the College of Liberal Arts & Sciences, which has about eight buildings, had their poll in the library.

After my close defeat, I was devastated, and almost felt like I had let everyone down. People had expected me to win, and when they heard that I had won the first election, didn't understand that there would be a run-off. So voting totals were down, and my opponent eked out a victory.

This loss made me realize that I had to be strong and confident and that things happen for a reason. I see now that this failure strengthened me and made my victory the next two years even more meaningful.

Choose a running mate. At USF, candidates run as a ticket so my most critical decision was to choose a running mate, someone who I felt was qualified to be vice president and president if I had to resign or couldn't complete my term. I wanted to run with someone who was a proven campus leader, easy to work with, and had an outgoing personality. I wanted someone who was committed to the issues and who had the drive and perseverance to overcome obstacles that probably would appear.

I chose Alisa Cooney, a peer in the College of Mass Communications and a very good friend. We had served as orientation leaders together and she was the president of the Panhellenic Council. She possessed strong leadership abilities and was an accomplished speaker. I had been advised to choose a student from another college to assure support in two Colleges, but I chose the person I felt was most qualified.

Develop an action plan and goals. Once you choose a running mate, next you should develop an action plan and realistic goals that include a platform of ideas, advertising and promotional strategies, a plan on how you'll recruit volunteers, and a budget. At USF, campaign budgets are limited to $1,100, and we spent about $750 per campaign. The run-off elections, on the other hand, have a $250 limit and we spent all of that.

Alisa and I were among nine tickets vying for the top SG jobs in Spring 1994. With a turnout in the election of 1,399 voters, we got 365 or 26 percent. In the run-off election, we won with 507 votes to 320 for the contenders. During the spring 1995 election, four tickets ran and about 1,200 student voted. In the close run-off, our ticket garnered 632 votes to 566 for the competition.

I believe I won my second election because we had never been in SG before, which was to our advantage because SG not long before had been shut down. But we had been leaders on campus—I was in charge of Homecoming, while Alisa was

Panhellenic president. We also weren't political science or pre-law majors, so I think students saw us as coming from a different mold.

It's pretty clear that we won my third campaign because we were widely recognized on campus, and had proven our leadership capabilities. We also had run two times previously and had learned what worked and what didn't.

Come up with clever advertising ideas. We devised many different promotional mechanisms to get our names out. One effective strategy was creating a campaign slogan, which for our first campaign was "No slogan, No gimmick, Just hard work." The second year, we focused on drawing attention to the past year's success, hence "Just DQ It Again!" Slogans definitely will give your campaign recognition, as students will see and hear it frequently, which will help their recall on ballot day.

During our first campaign, we borrowed a button maker, then later bought one for the reelection bid. Volunteers helped make buttons, and letter and paint signs, often on the front lawn of my parents' home. Campaign workers, including me and Alisa, designed flyers and posted them around campus.

We attempted to make all our flyers and publicity creative and eye-catching. For example, we bought tiny envelopes to be distributed all over campus. Each envelope was stamped with "confidential" in red with the goal of appealing to students' curiosity. The technique worked as students readily took the envelopes, tore them open, and found the greeting "Vote DQ and Alisa" on a card along with directions to all of the voting locations. Not only were students intrigued, but many immediately went to the polls to vote.

We also attribute many votes to our friends who turned their cars into moving billboards for our campaign. During the week before the election, close to 400 cars were shoe-polished with "DQ and Alisa." Our goal was to bombard students, which we hoped would translate in better name recognition when students went to the polls.

Another type of flyer we used was a "door knocker." Around

Vice President-elect Cooney and President-elect Quilleon take the oath of office from Kimberly Constantine, Chief Justice of the USF Supreme Court.

3:30 a.m. the night before the election, Alisa and I, along with about 30 of our faithful volunteers, delivered these flyers with the phrase "Good morning! Don't forget to vote today for DQ and Alisa." We posted these on doors and cars at nearby apartments, since USF doesn't have a lot of on-campus housing. For the residence halls, we posted the flyers on bikes outside. We also put flyers on cars at nearby bars. You have to get permission to post flyers on campus, while you don't off-campus.

Speak to student groups. Alisa and I spoke to many student groups by calling ahead and making appointments to attend their meetings— this is a valid method both to attract voters and help students understand our reasons for seeking SG positions. If we weren't able to schedule an appearance, we recruited a member of the organization to speak for us. During these brief talks, usually about five minutes at the beginning of the meeting, we identified specific ways that students could get involved in our campaign and presented our carefully constructed goals for our administration. We also answered questions right then and gave our home phone numbers to each group president should a member have a question or concern later. I had noticed that some previous candidates take themselves way too seriously and we wanted to show that we would be available to every student at all times.

On election day, Alisa and I made appearances at the different Colleges reminding students to vote and thanking those who had. Two years ago, e-mail wasn't that big at USF, but it was in the Engineering College, so we posted e-mail messages to all of the engineering students, encouraging them to vote and vote for us. Our parents even came to campus to help us pass out flyers. Since USF is a predominantly commuter campus and many of our students are above the traditional age, having our moms campaigning was very successful. The last election was held on rainy days, but my undaunted Mom stood in front of the College of Business with her bright red umbrella emblazoned with "Vote DQ and Alisa." We more than doubled our votes from the year before at that College. Mom also campaigned in front of the Phyllis Marshall Center, the main student union.

Don't be afraid to debate. Campus debates also were an important part of the election process. Although the debates weren't well attended, we always had a core group of about 45 students there. The debates were held in the open near the student center and students frequently paused to listen on the way to class. At first we thought the debates were a waste of time. However, they were featured prominently in the campus paper, *The Oracle*, the following day. I think the debates helped the newspaper to report on what the candidates stood for and allowed the readers to get a better idea of who the candidates were and how they presented themselves.

Alisa and I went out "on the town" almost every night before the election. We went where we knew we would see other USF students, including bars, dining halls, dance clubs, and popular Ybor City night spots. By interacting with our peers on a social level, they were able to see that we were real students.

My campaign's success was dependent on delegating duties to others. If you can motivate students to help and be part of your campaign, then you'll probably be successful later at motivating them to get involved in campus issues.

The challenge is being sincere and genuine in your campaign. I worked diligently, recruited excellent staff, and committed myself to working with all Student Government entities to make an SG that USF students could be proud of. During my terms of office, SG made recommendations to use Capital Improvement Trust Funds to build the first campus high-rise parking garage, beautify the Martin Luther King Plaza, and make $6 million in renovations to residence halls. Student Government also was a leading force in preventing the popular Cresent Hill from being used to build the new parking garage. I also advocated that a football program be started for USF at a State Board of Regents meeting — and today USF has a fledgling football program. In March 1996 as my final term was ending, the statewide magazine *Florida Leader* recognized USF's Student Government as the best in the state.

I sought the SG president position because I wanted to make a positive contribution to my university. For my commitment, I have a wealth of invaluable experience, lifetime friendships, and an appreciation for the opportunities that USF enabled me to enjoy. The skills I learned through the SG experience are a wonderful bonus to the degree I also earned.

Contact: David M. Quilleon
Address: 7410 Key Colony Ave., #2025,
Winter Park, FL 32792
Phone: (407) 673-0474
Fax: (407) 898-1281
E-mail: dquil@aol.com

A Diverse Team Wins At Florida State University

By Liza Park
1996-97 Student Government President
Florida State University

Introduction

In addition to serving as SG president, Park, 25, was president of Delta Zeta sorority and of the Lady Spirithunters and was co-founder of Burning Spear, a leadership organization. In 1995, she was one of seven finalists for the Florida College Student of the Year Award.

Park will graduate from the Florida State University School of Law in Spring 1998.

How Park Learned From the Past To Win At FSU

The state Capitol Building is next door to the FSU campus, and often the politics and passions of the Florida legislature trickle down to our Student Government influencing campus politics, issues, and the political structure.

FSU's SG closely resembles state and national governments, with executive, legislative, and judicial branches as well as agencies, bureaus, affiliated projects, departments, a full cabinet, funding boards, a recreation board, a union board, a Senior Class Council, and the Congress of Graduate Students. Much like real-world government, FSU's SG tends to be dominated by political parties that influence decisions and election outcomes and form strong alliances among members. The party-driven system also creates divisive social, philosophical, and political ditches among the parties and their members.

Combine these factors with a $5.3 million budget, powerful special-interest groups, 30,000 students, and a couple of independent student newspapers, and the result is one extremely serious student government. To run for FSU student body president and to serve in this office is, quite frankly, the greatest preparation imaginable for the rigors of real politics.

Once you understand your own SG's structure and continue to evaluate whether to run, honestly ask yourself these questions: "Why do I want to be student body president? Why should I be president? Am I the very best candidate for the job?" Also ask "Do I really want to go through the stress? What are my chances? How will I get there?" It's in your best interest and your student body's to answer these questions before throwing your hat into the presidential ring.

The next question an FSU candidate needs to answer is "Who should be my running mate?" Here, presidential and vice presidential candidates must run together on one ticket, so your vice president should share your vision and goals for SG. Just like on a national level, your partner should be someone who represents substantial constituencies and voting blocks across campus — preferably different groups than your own.

For example, my vice president, Wayne Messam, was a major figure in the African-American community and with student athletes. He was active in his fraternity and in the Black Student Union and was a starting wide receiver for the Seminole football team. On the other hand, I had been involved in the predominately white Greek system, a few of the Asian student groups, and several leadership and service organizations. I also had served as president for some of those groups, was a two-term SG senator, and was a first-year law student.

Because of our high-profile involvement on campus, Wayne and I had fairly widespread name recognition. More importantly, we represented a large portion of FSU students, more so than the other two opposing tickets. One of the other tickets was represented by two white, male Greeks who traveled in the same circles. One candidate had lots of SG experience, while the other had held Greek leadership positions. Their weakness was that both appealed to the same constituency. The other ticket was com-

The O.N.L.Y.
SOLUTIONS

You Complained . . . We Listened

You said you want us to . . .

- FORCE PARKING REFORM
- OFFER FREE E-MAIL FOR EVERYONE
- INCREASE MINORITY REPRESENTATION IN SGA
- EXTEND DROP AND ADD WINDOW
- INCREASE CRIME PREVENTION MEASURES
- IMPLEMENT A 3-STEP PLAN FOR A SAFER TENNESSEE ST.
- PIONEER ON-LINE CLASS REGISTRATION
- UPGRADE RESIDENCE HALL LIVING CONDITIONS
- IMPROVE ACADEMIC ADVISING
- INCREASE WEEKEND COMPUTER LAB HOURS
- END THE MARRIOTT MONOPOLY
- EXPAND STUDENT PUBLIC ACCESS/ FSU CHANNEL 47
- EXTEND LEACH CENTER HOURS
- INSTALL A REALISTIC RECYCLING PROGRAM
- MAINTAIN PERMANENT "PLEASE COMPLAIN" HOTLINE

Vote Park / Messam, Wednesday February 28th

Park's plethora of campaign literature included a detailed platform flyer, which featured the logo at the top right. The logo was made into buttons and stickers as well.

posed of a black male and a white female who had some SG experience. However, neither one had strong ties or memberships with any particular campus group.

Our ticket was a sign of the times. We became the first minority ticket to have a legitimate chance to win. One of the hot issues was minority representation, so our ethnic heritage undoubtedly helped us. Compelled to bring a voice for minorities to SG, Wayne had already made up his mind to run for vice president. Mutual friends who had been involved with student politics introduced us, and we exchanged ideas. We had compatible personalities, similar concerns, and the same vision for a more equitable SG.

Learn about past races. As in real politics, you should review the voting history of previous winners. At Florida State, even though all students, including law, graduate, and doctoral students, can vote and run in SG elections, mostly undergraduates participate. The average voter turnout is about 10 percent of the student body, or 3,500 voters, a large portion of which are Greeks.

By studying the previous year's results, we learned that 3,300 students voted for five different tickets. Nobody won a majority in the general election, so the top two tickets went into a runoff. In both of the two previous years, the runoffs were between two separate, Greek-based tickets. We knew we needed more than just Greek support to win outright, especially because one of the two tickets in our race was primarily Greek.

To do this, we needed a very broad base of supporters. We hoped to pull in some minority students, as well as Greeks, non-Greeks, and older students. As it turned out, that's exactly what happened, and by targeting a broader voter base, we won and increased turnout by almost 1,000 votes. With more than 4,200 students voting, Wayne and I were able to avoid a runoff by winning outright with a little more than 51 percent.

Build a party. In previous years, the winning candidates ran with a party. No one could remember any independent candidates winning the presidency without party support. Therefore, although Wayne and I originally thought about running independently, we faced the facts and ran with a party. However, because neither one of us felt comfortable with any existing parties, we decided to start one.

With the help of former student body president Sean Pittman, Wayne and I and a few of our closest friends formed the O.N.L.Y. (Outstanding New Leadership for You) Party. We found lots of immediate support because we planned, not promised, to remedy the complaints students had about existing parties. Some students said existing political parties were too social and one-sided. One was composed of white Greeks, another was comprised of African-American students, and the other had an image of being radical graduate students. Additionally, students said that they couldn't easily tell what each party wanted to accomplish.

We identified the principles of our party upfront — "diversity, professionalism, and ethics" — and promoted them in every advertisement, flyer, and speaking engagement. Before Wayne and I went public with the new party idea, we tried to sell it to the African-American based party and Greek leaders. We created a "core" group that would be the new party's leadership, made up of people who wanted us to win just as if they were running themselves. A solid core will direct, lead, and carry a new party. In our case, we had the talent and credibility of several top student leaders, past and present, from the most active, diverse, and visible student groups on campus.

Know your opponents. Knowing whom you will be running against is key in planning your campaign and sometimes can determine if you should even run. If you already know that a potential opponent is someone who would do a fantastic job and would command lots of support, think twice about running. However, if you feel that you can do a better job than anyone else, go for it. A good president understands students, has a vision, can execute a plan, and embodies the spirit of the school. To win, you've got to show that you can do all this better than your opponents.

You'll also want to distinguish yourself from the opposi-

Park ran with football player and activist Wayne Messam, a combination which became the first "all-minority" ticket to win the top two elected SG positions at FSU.

tion, know what she is like, who her staunch supporters will be, and why. This will help you identify voters who will automatically support your opposition and those who might support you. Once this is established, spend most of your time targeting those in-between students and groups whose votes are up for grabs, as well as maintaining your stronghold of supporters.

Know the rules. Taking time to understand election rules will be some of the best-spent hours of your campaign. It's a must here at FSU. There are specific requirements and limitations as to what you can or cannot do before the official active campaigning time commences. If you aren't familiar with the election code, it's all too easy to be in violation before you even announce your candidacy.

To be on the safe side, Wayne and I studied our elaborate election code over the 1995 holiday break. This gave us a working knowledge of the rules before anyone knew about our new party or our bid for office. We also needed to know the code, because it defines campaigning spending limits.

At the time we ran, each presidential ticket could spend up

to $3,000 during the week of active campaigning, including any donated materials. However, this was only the amount limit for the week prior to the actual election day. You could promote the party before active campaigning week, but you couldn't promote yourself. General party expenditures didn't count toward the $3,000 limit.

Raising money and campaign budgeting. Because our limit is a rather large amount for any one student to come up with, fund raising is important. Wayne and I started our fundraising effort by sending letters to friends, family, and folks back home (past teachers, coaches, parents' associates). Our parents and friends donated some, and we held a few car washes to build up a financial base.

Before you move on with your campaign, get your finances straight. At Florida State, each ticket must have an official campaign treasurer. Choose someone who is competent, meticulous, and trustworthy.

Also, most campaigns have a campaign manager. Once these positions are established, the candidates, campaign manager(s), and treasurer(s) should set up a realistic budget for the entire campaign. This usually includes costs for active campaign week, advertisements, and meetings. Also account for buying brochures, notebooks, flyers, and food before active campaigning week, as well as campaign social events such as retreats and general promotional functions. A generous, realistic budget must be outlined and followed.

At Florida State, I've heard of past presidential campaigns costing as much as $10,000 and as little as a few hundred dollars. Yes, it's possible to "buy" a campaign, but it's also possible to lose with an expensive one. Planning and preparation are key, not frivolous and wasteful spending. My treasurer, Jane Dueease, who also became a campaign manager, was a fellow sorority sister and was fabulous. She documented every single expenditure right down to each paper clip and staple we used. She also designed almost every printed flyer, poster, and other literature, which eliminated design costs. She forced us to plan out all printing needs in advance, put in one mass order, and worked out deals with every vendor. This saved us at least $1,000.

When it was all over, our ticket won without the dreaded runoff and came in almost $1,000 under the campaign limit. We also spent about $1,000 less than our main competitor. However, our entire campaign appeared to be very professional because of great planning and budgeting.

Know the issues and believe in your platform. It seems strange that so far I've been talking about the campaign process rather than the issues, which are paramountly important here. FSU's SG president is much more than a figurehead. He or she also is a department director, the executive branch manager, the main voice for 30,000 students, a chief student lobbyist for higher education, and the one who holds veto power over all senate statutory and finance bills. Our SG president can approve more than $5.3 million in expenditures and budgets annually. During my term, I signed off on roughly $12 million for two budgets during the fiscal year.

Undoubtedly, our SG officials have the power to change and improve conditions on campus. However, you have to have a clear-cut plan to get there. It's essential that you know what the major issues and complaints on campus are, research them, and develop resolutions to solve those problems or to make improvements.

Each ticket typically compiles a list of between 10 and 20 platform planks. They state what the ticket wants to do for students, such as increase minority representation in SG or identify problem areas such as Homecoming and parking. Instead of guessing at what the students cared about most, Wayne and I conducted a month-and-a-half-long survey about SG, student life, and student services. We got advice from a couple of communication professors, and starting in early January, we had our staffers conduct a phone survey of every fourth student listed in the campus directory. This also was a way to build interest in the new party, because we let students know who was conducting the survey. After gathering hundreds of useful responses, we broadened the idea by creating a "Please Complain Campaign," because, in es-

As FSU SG president, Park spoke at the ceremony for the 1997 Florida College Student of the Year Award. She was one of only seven finalists in 1995.

sence, that's what we were asking people to do. We gathered complaints from all over campus, actually getting students who were normally apathetic to participate.

After compiling the data, Wayne and I had proof of what the students wanted. Our campaign platforms were based directly on the survey and hundreds of handwritten complaints from students.

On the campaign trail. The elections were in late February, and we had started building the O.N.L.Y. Party in mid-November. We spent all of December, even the holiday break, planning and building. We began advertising the coming of a new party on the first day of classes in January and had our first open meeting on the third week of the semester. Just as we had hoped, we attracted more than 200 students from a wide range of backgrounds for the first meeting. We were told by past presidents and party leaders that you can tell if you have a chance to win by the attendance at your opening meeting, the diversity of students, and the enthusiasm in the room.

You can never have too many volunteers. Our pool of volunteers increased overnight from just core members to literally hundreds of excited and energetic newcomers. Each person who takes the time to check out your meeting is important to your campaign. We had anticipated this influx of new faces and created a core officer to nurture new members. By the time we won our election, every volunteer in the O.N.L.Y. Party felt as though he or she had won. I think they cared more because they had been deeply involved in forming the party. That's the feeling of ownership you want to create. Two people don't just get into office — a whole wave of students wins.

You never can get too much good press. Student newspapers can provide great coverage if you design news to be of interest to the editors. Our news angle was the "Please Complain Campaign." The catchy name caught on quickly and students loved the idea of being asked to complain. The "Please Complain Campaign" grabbed a lot of media attention, making the local TV news and front page of the student papers, *The Florida Flambeau* and *FSView*. However, none of the coverage would have happened without making sure that press releases reached every media source available. In fact, we even held a press conference on the first day of active campaigning to reveal the results of the "Please Complain" survey. Both local TV stations and two radio stations showed up. The press conference was held at peak foot-traffic time in the middle of the student union, the largest polling site. The administration even became interested in the "Please Complain" and requested copies.

The one mandatory campaign debate was covered by the media as well, with front-page articles and photos one day before the election. Like at most schools, the debates aren't well attended. Mostly supporters and reporters showed for ours.

Neither of the two papers endorsed any ticket, although we got the most favorable advance press. Usually, *The Flambeau* endorses the radical candidate, but there wasn't one that year. An endorsement by *FSView* probably could have influenced the election. However, most of their advertising support comes from the Greek community, so the paper usually doesn't endorse any one

Greek ticket over another.

Other than free coverage from media sources, you also can advertise in the papers and on the radio. Wayne and I created our own radio ad for a popular local station that ran during the last three days of active campaigning. We also bought newspaper ads for the party for several weeks prior to the election. On election day, we printed our picture and platforms in an ad in both school newspapers. However, newspaper and radio ads can be expensive, so budget ahead of time.

Reach out to everyone. About three weeks away from the election, you should already be scheduled to speak at an event or to a group just about every day. Two weeks away, start speaking at two or three different organization meetings daily. And during the last few days before the election, go back to large organizations and blocks of traditionally heavy voters.

We had a scheduler look up meeting times and call contacts to ask if we could speak. Before active campaign time, we spoke to groups about the new party, but we couldn't talk about our personal candidacies. Overall, we probably spoke at 20 houses in the Greek community, made up of 17 sororities and 25 fraternities, and at another 20 groups including the Lady Spirithunters, all the athletic teams, the Fellowship of Christian Athletes, Student Alumni Association, and the Marching Chiefs.

Just remember that it's important that you connect with people and let them talk about themselves. Stay for their meetings to find out more about them. After all, if you want to be their president, you should really know the people you'll be representing. Their concerns should be your concerns. If you don't care, think twice about running.

Stay visible at the end. Your campaign will consist of a lot of paper, including flyers, posters, door hangers, yard signs, handbills, brochures, and newsletters. All of these have been important throughout the years in FSU campaigns. Our campaign utilized professional-looking picture posters of Wayne and me, our platforms on half-sheets with the picture poster design on the opposite side, O.N.L.Y. Party stickers, Park/Messam stickers, different flyers for each week since the O.N.L.Y. Party formed, generic O.N.L.Y flyers, newspaper ads, and radio spots. Everything was in red, white, and blue and usually included our logo. This doesn't have to be expensive if you plan ahead and do one mass printing order, but you must be organized.

Everything boils down to organization. While successful campaigns require hard work and determination, if you don't think beforehand and if you don't work smart, you'll find yourself looking at a loss. Planning, organization, and communication by you and your core staff will determine the caliber of your campaign.

Unlike some candidates who have elaborate victory bashes, we were a serious group from day one. Students were so sick of the "socialness" of SG, so we were "all business." All of the O.N.L.Y candidates and volunteers were happy to win, of course, but we weren't best buddies going out on the town together. We had issues that we cared about, which is what united us.

Listen, listen, work, and listen. It's been said that 90 percent of leadership is listening. Having served in numerous presidencies throughout my college career, I wholeheartedly agree. However, don't wait until you're elected to begin listening. A president isn't always a leader, and leaders don't always become president. As you approach your own bid for office, make sure that you are a good leader and a listener. Be attentive to your running mate, take advice from your core staff, and listen carefully to the needs of your student body. They're always saying something with their actions and behavior. To be able to listen and understand your constituents is the best quality you can possess as a student leader. And leadership is simply the opportunity to serve.

Contact: Liza Park
Address: 836-B Georgia St., Tallahassee, FL 32304

Friend-To-Friend Campaign Yields Victory At the University of Hawaii

By Scott Y. Nishimoto
1996-97 Associated Students President
University of Hawaii at Manoa

Introduction

Nishimoto, 23, majored in sociology and is a member of Alpha Kappa Beta, Golden Key Honor Society, and the Students in American Studies organization. He spent a summer as a congressional intern for Sen. Daniel K. Inouye (Dem-HI) in Washington, D.C.

After graduating in May 1997, Nishimoto was selected as a Fellow with the Congressional Asian-Pacific American Caucus Institute in Washington, D.C.

How Nishimoto Campaigned Year-Round To Win

Before I ran for office, as a senator-at-large and then as president of ASUH, I knew I would have to combat the commuter-student lifestyle and their limited involvement in campus activities. Because of this, I felt I had to garner votes from those who knew me personally.

This was especially important, because historically, not even 20 percent of UHM students vote in student government elections. Here, it's more who you know and how many friends you can convince to vote. So I really didn't need to have a formal platform, although I did want to get more students involved in campus activities and give ASUH more visibility.

The University of Hawaii at Manoa (UHM) is a commuter campus with about 18,000 students; undergraduates account for 12,000 of this total. Hawaii residents comprise 87 percent of UHM students, and most of them drive to school for classes and leave when they're done. Twenty-five percent of our students are 30 years or older. There's also no ethnic majority, which explains why UHM has been labeled as a "rainbow" student body. I myself am Asian.

I was up against two other candidates. One was the current ASUH vice president who was active in the Filipino Club, while the other was a native Hawaiian student who didn't have previous ASUH experience.

While candidates can announce their intentions to run early, there's a formal two-week campaign period. Unlike many schools, Greek groups don't always dominate campus politics. Some years the entire senate is Greek, but it's not consistently like this. My vice presidential running mate was a fraternity member, so I'm sure that some of my support came from the Greek community.

My Little Black Book. After I decided to run, I identified and listed everyone I knew on campus. This was an ongoing activity throughout the school year. Each time I came across someone I knew, I told him or her of my candidacy, got a current phone number, and asked for a pledge of support. I recruited about 20 friends to help out with the campaign through these calls. Plus, the list later proved to be my main approach: the "friend-to-friend" campaign of counting my votes.

Walking the Territory. As soon as I had the green light to actively campaign two weeks before the election, I went door-to-door at the student housing complex which is home to approximately 2,000 students, including myself. These students were primarily from neighboring islands. Rather than walking in alone, I enlisted residents of a particular dorm to take me to the rooms where their friends lived to introduce me. I took flyers and business cards announcing my candidacy with the theme, "Working for a Better University." After meeting me, some students offered to post my flyer on their dorms or apartment windows to help with campaign advertising.

In assessing the door-to-door technique, I can't actually say it resulted in more votes. While I think it might have helped, I have nothing concrete to back up this feeling. I do know that it involved a lot of delicate arrangements. I had to set up appointment times for each informal "campaign manager" to take me around. We found the late evening hours between 10 p.m. and midnight worked best, as students usually were available during those times. On a good evening, I was able to shake hands and chat with 20 students.

I did some cold calling on my own but found that knocking on doors without someone to say "Hey, I want you to meet this guy who is running for ASUH President" was equivalent to pounding the pavement to sell insurance policies to strangers. It meant doors were either not opened or they weren't open for very long. So again, the idea of friend-to-friend seemed to work.

Scott
Nishimoto
FOR ASUH PRESIDENT
Elections: April 9, 10, 11

"Working for a better university"

snishimo@hawaii.edu   *957-1771*

Nishimoto handed out this "business card" to students he met when campaigning across campus.

Based on feedback I got, campaigning in this fashion was a first on our campus and showed I was serious and committed to the election. It was easy and routine to just post flyers around campus and speak at arranged forums. But my efforts in going beyond these traditional campaign tactics were acknowledged as noteworthy.

Since I focused on making personal contact with potential voters, I didn't speak at a lot of student group meetings, even though we have about 300 clubs on campus. I did go out of my way to talk with members of the Pre-Law Society, a group of about 40 very likely voters.

The paper blitz. Lastly, I worked the campaign using traditional modes of publicity such as posting flyers all over campus. This approach was used by all candidates, so it was well-regulated. We had only certain bulletin boards that could be used. Knowing that students would see tons of electoral flyers, I de-

Scott

Nishimoto
FOR ASUH PRESIDENT
Elections: April 9, 10, 11
"Working for a better university"

March 15, 1996

Dear Student Organization,

Please allow me to introduce myself. My name is Scott Y. Nishimoto and I currently hold the position of Senator-At-Large within ASUH. Presently, I am a candidate for the position of President within ASUH, and would like to invite your views and ideas on the University. Please feel free to contact me at home, 957-1771.

I consider Registered Independent Organizations(RIO's) an important component of the college experience for students and would like to see their continued participation in campus life. As a Senator, I have been very interested in RIO funding and have voted for increased funding for organizations. As the State of Hawaii and the University of Hawaii face uncertain budgets, I am committed to maintaining and, if possible increasing RIO funding from present levels so that involvement in programs and activities can be maintained.

I would like to encourage you to vote April 9, 10, and 11.

Sincerely yours,

Scott Y. Nishimoto

Scott Y. Nishimoto
ASUH Senator-At-Large

cided to get the edge by selecting a non-traditional paper size of 11" x 17" instead of 8 1/2" x 11" — advice I got from a former ASUH president. I also selected a thicker poster paper in bright, fluorescent colors and used this in select places like glass-covered bulletin boards or enclosed buildings where my flyers wouldn't be trashed. For public bulletin boards, I used white 11" x 17" paper. I think including my picture helped promote me as a real student, not just a name.

I also designed some campaign business cards to pass out. To accompany the business cards, we wrote letters to all student organizations and mailed the materials to their leaders' home addresses.

With a spending limit of $500, partly because of cost constraints, I was against running ads in the school paper. I also thought running flashy ads would hurt more than help. Candidates who had done it in the past were met with mixed results. I think a lot of students believe that means you're a slick candidate if you do this, so there's some negative backlash. I purposely kept my promotional materials simple.

Counting the sure votes. I called upon my little black book heavily in the last two weeks of the campaign. I called to remind each person on the list about the coming election, particularly the dates, times, and polling places. I asked students with solid networks of friends to contact at least five of them personally. I suggested five, because I knew that even if they contacted just one friend, it meant a potential voter who would go the extra mile if asked by a friend.

While I was working the phone lines, I made sure to talk to students on issues and concerns. Although I knew that winning an election at UHM centered more on who you knew than on platforms and promises, I was very aware of vision, direction, and problems. Being elected was one thing, but coming through once elected was part of the package deal.

I chose to be a realist more than a visionary. I didn't make lofty promises, because I felt I couldn't compromise my credibility against the budget-crunching times the university was facing. I stressed quality, maintenance, and efficiency with no backpedaling as far as student rights and interests were concerned. My feeling was, "Why lose ground being a battering ram against a stone wall?"

The focus on spring. At UHM, student government elections are held during the second week of April. Early on, I decided that the friend-to-friend concept would work better if I were enrolled in small classes. I also picked an array that included courses outside of my major. As it turned out, the small classes allowed me to interact with fellow students, and I got a few to assist in my campaign.

Even the times of my classes played an important part during this semester. When possible, I avoided courses offered in the early morning when students commute and also during lunch hour. I used those times to campaign by passing out flyers and business cards at the parking structure and at walkways between the dorms and the main campus.

Thankfully, throughout the campaign and my term of office, I was able to work ahead on my course work, so I didn't have to miss many classes or tests. In fact, I graduated with a 3.6 G.P.A.

Along with deliberate class choices for the semester, I again chose to live at the UHM Student Housing Complex just as I had my freshman year. I knew that I needed to capitalize on the dormitory population for potential votes. I also felt comfortable reaching out to them as I was a veteran resident.

Instead of having a debate, all three candidates appeared at an open forum which was taped by our Student Video Association. Our speeches then were replayed on VCRs in key locations on campus, such as at the cafeterias. As a result, a lot of people saw the forum, even though the actual event was attended by only 40 students, most of whom were our supporters.

Our campus daily, *The Ka Leo O Hawaii*, didn't openly endorse any candidate, but in effect, the paper favored my opponent with glowing articles about her for weeks leading up to the election. This was subtle to the average student but noted by campus political insiders as an annual tradition.

When the results were announced, I garnered 230 votes, 80 more than my closest opponent. The total voter turnout of about 500 was similar to past years. I was recovering from the campaign in my dorm room when I learned that I had won. It took a while for it to sink in since I was so tired. At the time, more than anything, I was just glad it was over.

When I look back at my term in office, I think student participation did go up a little bit and ASUH was more visible this year. There were more articles in the paper about us and I did a commercial that ran statewide for the University to recruit high school students. We also did well at the legislature this year and got a bill passed to put a voting student member on the Board of Regents. We've been trying to accomplish this goal for 15 years. We lobbied and testified, and lawmakers now are taking students seriously. We also got construction started on an addition to our library.

In hindsight, I won because I built my campaign around those I could rely on to extend my network. I researched previous elections and knew the voters who bothered to cast ballots did so because they knew someone. To that end, I organized my efforts by taking the direct and personalized route: person-to-person, friend-to-friend campaigning.

Contact: Scott Nishimoto
Address: 94-210 Mahinahou Place, Mililani, HI 96789
Phone: (808) 623-3340

An Insider Battles Apathy To Win At The University of Iowa

By Allison Miller
1997-98 University of Iowa Student Government President
University of Iowa

Introduction

Miller, 21, started a program to promote non-alcoholic events, organized lobbying trips, and created the university's first Freshman Council.

In addition, Miller has been campus director of the United Students of Iowa, residence hall vice president and secretary, and an information desk worker. As a junior in political science, Miller hasn't decided on her plans after graduation in May 1998.

An Insider Overcomes Politicking To Win

Being the insider actually made things harder when I ran for UISG president. Almost immediately after I was elected as Undergraduate Activities Senate (UAS) Executive, seven months before the March 1997 elections, fellow students started asking if I wanted to be president. I thought it was crazy to predict that far in advance, but soon I found it hard to stop thinking about that possibility. I reasoned that the sooner I decided, the better prepared I'd be.

So in September 1996, I spoke with Meghan Henry, my coworker, friend, and current Undergraduate Collegiate Senate (UCS) Executive, about running together. As executives in both undergraduate senates, we had an extensive knowledge of UISG, had worked with every student group on campus, and had networked with administrators and community and state leaders. With Meghan and me on the same ticket, very few students were willing to run against us.

The favorites become targets. On a campus where most students don't think UISG does anything, let alone anything for them, we were hit with waves of criticism from the campus and local newspapers as well as our opponent. We were criticized for being paid, for not communicating with students, for sympathizing with the administration, and for being resume builders. It didn't seem to matter that we created programs used by thousands of students.

After getting this unwarranted criticism, our spirits were pretty low. What kept us going was the fact we had a record of accomplishments. Over time, we showed why our extensive involvement should be a primary reason why students should elect us: we could go straight to work with little training or downtime.

Because potential opponents knew Meghan and I would make a formidable ticket, they made many attempts to split us. Meghan and I allowed ourselves to be courted by opponents who hoped we might switch sides, all the while knowing we wouldn't switch tickets.

This posturing merely served as a tool to get information. We learned that if we ran, others might change their plans, so we stayed quiet until all eight members of our ticket were ready to come forward in full force. We wanted a team of campus leaders who could work well together and have a high level of trust, because we knew this was going to be a tough race. This full ticket put our campaign spending limit at $3,500. One of my family members donated the money, but I'm confident we could have raised enough if necessary. I was lucky not to have to worry about fundraising, because it allowed us to start planning sooner.

Know your opponent. I ran against one of my best friends, Chad Doellinger, president of the Associated Residence Halls, who had worked alongside me for the past three years. I had been in the same hall government with him for two years, had worked at one of the residence hall info desks, and had served as a residence hall senator for two years.

Since my opponent didn't have a full ticket, he couldn't raise as much money and didn't have as large a network of potential voters or volunteers.

Planning ahead. Right after winter break in early January, we met twice a week, which created a close-knit group. During these meetings, we came up with our 10-point platform and picked our campaign picture, flyer and poster designs, and color scheme. After a three-hour brainstorming meeting, we finally decided on our slogan, "It's All About Students."

Choosing a platform. Each of our eight ticket members had such varied leadership experience, that we felt like we had expert knowledge about dozens of important issues. However, the only major difference between our platform and our opponents' was we had been working on many issues for two years. Our angle was to show the media and student body that it takes years to get things done on campus, especially policy changes. I constantly talked about what a mistake it would be to start over from scratch.

Spreading the word. We knew that most of Chad's votes would come from the residence halls, so we blanketed them with flyers, while following a very strict set of posting rules. There are guidelines about when, where, and for how long posters can be displayed. We had posters in every building and hallway. We also put flyers on the doors of all hall residents who supported us. In addition, we made quarter-sheet flyers to hand out at the residence hall dinner lines the week before the election. These flyers had a group picture on one side and our platform issues on the other, along with the ticket name and slogan.

On the other hand, Chad only made brochures. He didn't have T-shirts, buttons, or anything else. His brochure included a lot of information, but most students glanced at it for about five seconds and trashed it.

We also hung flyers in the stores and bars around town in Iowa City and asked managers to hang the posters in break rooms, since many employees are students. We also blanketed the outside kiosks in the city. They're four-sided bulletin boards, and anyone can put up flyers on them.

Posters aren't allowed anywhere on campus except bulletin

boards — and we're not even allowed to put the posters up ourselves. We give them to a central office, which then gives the flyers to contacts in each building, who then put them up. Because the on-campus bulletin boards are so crowded, we really didn't make them a central part of our strategy.

We handed out T-shirts to ticket supporters to wear on election days, because all other advertising had to be taken down then. No campaigning is allowed at all on the two election days, but if your message is on a shirt or button on "your person," it is permitted. We also reached hundreds of students through e-mail, reminding them to vote for us. We sent e-mail to the mailing lists of groups that didn't have meetings during the campaign, and we got their permission before sending the letters. We also set up decorated tables in the student union and handed out flyers for two days.

I even randomly called about 25 students listed in the University's phone book to tell them about the ticket and to encourage them to vote. Sometimes, when I wasn't scheduled to be at a meeting or speak to a group, I picked up the phone book and called students I didn't know. I felt like I needed to be doing something to help the campaign at all times.

Speak to groups. We attended every residence hall meeting, almost always on the same night as Chad, because the groups had only one meeting before the election. I liked it when both tickets were there at the same time, because students easily could see the differences between us.

Before we spoke at any group meeting or event, we made tons of phone calls the night before to encourage students to come and bring their friends for free pizza. Giving away pizzas helped us get students to stay in one place long enough to talk to them. We took the pies to every meeting, but we never had enough. The groups' leaders would tell us to expect 20 attendees, then 50 would show up. Some students would say, "I can't believe you're buying your votes," but they came and listened anyway.

An innovative marketing idea. We made a deal with the largest pizza delivery business in town at no cost to us. Since we

The Miller / Henry Ticket

It's All About Students

☆ Equitable English Proficiency Standards ☆

☆ Published Course Evaluations ☆

☆ Debit Card for Dining ☆

☆ Assault Prevention ☆

☆ Dead Week ☆

Polling Sites:
Mayflower
Burge
Quadrangle
Fieldhouse
IMU
Pappajohn
Van Allen
...and more!

Vote March 3 & 4 --
Student Government Presidential Elections!!

Miller's ticket designed posters and handbills which included the slogan "It's All About Students" and put them on top of pizza boxes delivered to students on and off campus.

were ordering around 10 pizzas for each meeting, we asked for a discount. Then we asked the business owner to let us tape our flyers to the tops of the pizza boxes sent out during their regular deliveries throughout the city and university. Not only did we hit the residence halls again, but we reached off-campus students who otherwise might not hear anything about the election. We also specifically asked that the other ticket not be allowed the same opportunity, and they agreed. We were the first to ever try this, and I think the owners respected that. Later, dozens of students told me they saw our flyers on the pizza boxes. It was one of the smartest moves we made and definitely the easiest.

Working the media. The two city papers, *The Iowa City Press Citizen* and *The Cedar Rapids Gazette*, did extensive articles and profiles of the two tickets, but neither is read by many students. *The Daily Iowan*, the morning Iowa City paper which is university-run, helped the most. The paper doesn't endorse particular candidates, but its front-page coverage during the campaign generated some name recognition for our ticket.

Most of the 28,000 students pick up a *Daily Iowan* every morning, and all residence hall students get copies delivered to their doors. We took advantage of that by spending over half of our campaign budget on a series of half-page ads featuring the ticket name, slogan, and photo. We designed all ads to stand out so they could be read quickly. Our final ad only had a simple message: "Don't forget to vote!"

Our most effective ad was a half-page list of 350 students who supported our ticket. Not only did students stop to look at the ad to see if they knew anybody listed, but supporters told their friends. In essence, it created an unending network of students who knew students who knew someone on the ticket and would vote for us.

Miller's ticket members: (Top) Anselm Efe and Anitra Hutcherson; (Middle) Erin Studer, Meghan Henry, John Craiger, and Josh Timmers; (Bottom) Miller and Janelle Johnson.

Our opponents ran only two small, text-heavy ads which were placed on a page opposite ours in the paper.

Focus on your strengths. We solicited the support of 25 to 30 large groups in which our opponents didn't have strong connections, including the Greek system, academic student groups, minority and religious groups, the Graduate Student Union, and organizations such as the Freshman Council, Student Video Productions, and Environmental Coalition. We had been working with these groups all year.

We never asked for public endorsements, mainly because we didn't think that anybody would vote for us because of a particular group's support. However, we knew that with club leaders on our side, we could count on their organizations' help. We also put flyers in law school students' mail boxes. In addition, we tried to make appearances at any UI event and even had ticket members attend the Sesquicentennial Ball in period costumes.

Every function was a chance to have one more quote or picture in the paper, meet one more professor who could announce the election in class, or contact one more student who hadn't met us yet. Any mention of the candidates in *The Daily Iowan*, whether directly related to the election or not, was free publicity for our ticket.

I wish we could have visited more of the 23 Greek houses. But every chapter meeting was on either Sunday or Monday night, so we had to be creative. When we couldn't make it, we asked house members to talk about our ticket and hand out flyers. It was more effective when a house member spoke on our behalf instead of a student not on the ticket or in the house.

Luckily, we were able to reach every house president at the IFC/Panhellenic Council meeting. As it turned out, it was the house president who often spoke for us. Finally, we attended house dinners, mostly in the sororities that had large dinner attendance and found this was an easy time to talk to a captive audience.

Recruiting volunteers. I really don't know how many students helped out. At one point, we had a fraternity pledge class hanging up our posters, and on election days, close to 100 students were campaigning for us at the end of their classes.

Delegation was easy, even though I started off paranoid that if I don't do it, it might not get done. Soon, though, I was calling people I hadn't spoken to since my freshman year and others I had met only once, but who seemed flattered that I had thought of them.

With two weeks to campaign, our ticket used the petitioning procedure to get our name out. Even though each ticket needed only 500 signatures to be on the ballot, we kept talking to students and getting their signatures, which was a way to "campaign" since the official campaign hadn't begun.

The debates. This isn't a turning point in our elections. Not surprisingly, a mere 28 students showed up. Only the presidential and vice presidential candidates participate and answer questions from a panel of students, faculty, and student representatives. With such a strong ticket, I didn't have to side-step any questions. I knew it was impossible for me to know every little thing about the university, but someone on my ticket did. Despite this confidence, we spent hours going over possible questions and even went up to the room the day of the debate to practice our opening and closing remarks at the podium and to get comfortable with the room's set-up.

The Daily Iowan and *The Press Citizen* both covered the debate. *The Daily Iowan* published a front-page article before and after the event, but these articles may have been overshadowed by the paper's editorials about student apathy. After the debate, every article blasted the indifference toward campus elections. The coverage focused on the candidates' inability to reach more students, which added to our frustration. We hadn't been sleeping, going to many classes, or thinking about anything else. Didn't students see us on campus? We had to be confident that they were.

The debate attendance numbers gave us an ominous taste of what election turnout numbers could look like.

And the winner is... Traditionally, the results are announced after a senate meeting outside the UISG office in the Iowa Memorial Union, so there were a lot of students and reporters milling around. I cringed when they asked Chad and me to go with the Elections Board into a little room. I came out stunned — only 7.37 percent or 1,917 students voted out of a total enrollment of 28,000, which was a typical turnout. Thankfully, the Miller/Henry Ticket got 1,417 votes or 74 percent, which was reported in the press as a "landslide." It was bittersweet to win with so few students seeming to care, but we were comforted knowing we'd have another year to put things on the right track.

Nothing slowed down after the election was over. I was weeks behind and had skipped almost every class that didn't have an attendance requirement. I did speak with my teachers before disappearing, and they all were stern but supportive. To top it off, mid-terms were during campaigning, so my grades were already slumping. I did take a lighter class load and plan to take fewer classes while I'm in office to give myself enough time. It's really a choice — if I had studied more during the campaign and slept even less, I might have earned better grades. But if I had done anything less, I might have lost, and I would never have forgiven myself.

Summary. I never had a grand plan for being student body president. I was the first woman UISG president at the University of Iowa, but that wasn't an issue during the campaign. I wanted to be elected based on abilities, not gender, so I focused on my experience and my record to attract voters.

Two years ago, I wouldn't have run at all. I had watched three administrations come and go, yet still happily asked for all of the stress, lack of sleep, and criticism that goes with campaigning. I wanted to do this, because I knew it would be one of the greatest experiences of my life. I also knew that I would regret not trying.

Contact: Allison Miller
Address: 12305 Francis Drake Drive,
Richmond, VA 23233
UISG's Web Address: http://www.uiowa.edu/~uisg

A Sophomore Outsider Wins At the University of Michigan

By Fiona Rose
1996-97 Michigan Student Assembly President
University of Michigan

Introduction

In her three years at the University of Michigan, Rose, 21, has rowed on the Women's Crew Team, played in the University Philharmonic Orchestra, and worked on community volunteer projects. Currently, she's a junior in classical archaeology and serves as the 1996-97 student body president.

After graduating in May 1998, Rose hopes to work in the public sector on education issues.

How Rose Learned from Defeat

Mine was a certain loss even before the final votes were cast. At 10 p.m., frantically passing out palm cards and pleas to harried students at the Graduate Library in the last minutes of the campaign, it slowly dawned on me: my bid for the vice presidency of the student body was for naught.

It was just a nagging feeling at the time; I knew that my running mate and I were underdogs. I was a freshman and naturally lacked the wide network of friends and contacts built up over the years by upperclassman candidates. My running mate hailed from the College of Engineering — a disadvantage when most student voters are part of a separate, larger college, the School of Literature, Science & Arts (LSA). Still, these factors alone did not ensure defeat. We lost the election because we lacked a message.

All the posters, T-shirts, and press releases in the world

couldn't have given our ticket a winning message. Garnering support from voters requires more than gimmicks, because students want real solutions to serious problems. I arrived at this conclusion after seeing letters to the editor in our campus newspaper and visiting with campus groups. Most students felt as if the Student Assembly was a joke, since previous administrations hadn't addressed their real needs. Because this is a campus of activists, if students vote, they're usually pretty savvy about the issues, attend the campaign debates, and write letters to the editor. Furthermore, with an increase in the number of non-traditional students comes an increase in demand for financial aid, health care, and provisions for dependants. These are needs historically neglected by major universities.

Make sure you understand voters. While young voters may not demand answers from their leaders to all of these issues, they do expect more than simple pleas for votes. In running for vice president, I failed to convince voters that I took their problems seriously and could be an effective advocate on their behalf. I also didn't understand our students and their concerns well enough, since my campaign was a "last-minute" decision. I had not had the chance to run in high school — my school didn't have a Student Government. I had been involved in local and state political campaigns as a volunteer, and I wanted to experience a campaign from the candidate's perspective.

Cognizant of this failure in my first campaign, I brushed off the frustration of defeat and readied myself for the next presidential race. Things would be different this time; I would be at the top of the ticket and would have a solid, persuasive message.

My career with the Michigan Student Assembly (MSA) — the sole central governing body for all 36,000 students on the University of Michigan's Ann Arbor Campus — began during my first semester in school as a first-year student.

While I didn't come to college intending to make student government the focus of my time and energy, my extracurricular activities easily opened that door to me. As a member of the crew team and as a musician in the University Philharmonic Orchestra, I had a ready-made base of support.

Furthermore, with many of my classes in large-lecture format, I had the advantage of reaching some 400 potential voters every time I stood up in class to ask for support. Using these connections, I ran for one of the highly contested LSA Representative positions and won with more votes than any other candidate.

After getting elected as a representative, I had nary a clue as to how or whom to lead. I learned the hard way, through trial and error, about the importance of poise, decisiveness, and thinking on one's feet. I threw myself into committee work and developed an intricate network of contacts in the student community. I also became aware of the power of the press.

Learn how to avoid being misquoted. UM's student newspaper, *The Michigan Daily*, is widely read and covers campus, state, national, and world news. Serving as a representative to the Assembly allowed me to test the media waters and learn how to avoid misquotes. Instead of just speaking off the cuff, I e-mailed quotations, wrote them down, or demanded the chance to review my quotations prior to publication before agreeing to be interviewed. I learned that you can contribute to a piece "on background" when the story is contentious.

Most importantly, however, contact with the press gave me free publicity. I have found that many busy student reporters are grateful for press releases and will often print them verbatim. Plus, writing one's own quotations into the press release is a guarantee against being misquoted. I learned the frustration of being misquoted early on. My freshman year, we announced our ticket first and a couple of weeks after that, the primary rival announced. My first reaction was, "Oh, I'm running against a couple of white males. It would be nice if we had a little more diversity." *The Daily* then reported in screaming headlines, "Rose blasts two white men." It painted me as an extremist, when in fact I'm pretty mainstream. It wasn't exactly that I was misquoted, but that I gave knee-jerk answers without thinking of how they could be interpreted. I also learned that I can call a reporter back instead of giving an immediate response — this gives you a chance to get your thoughts together before you say something that might come back to haunt you.

Putting in hours of work through three semesters on the Assembly as a representative readied me for a presidential run in my sophomore year: I had gained leadership abilities, communication skills, strong links to various student organizations, and a clearer vision of campus needs than I had as a freshman running for vice president.

I sized up the field: the race was comprised of six presidential tickets, with many candidates representing different factions. Three of the tickets could be automatically written off, as they featured political parties designed to appeal to very specific constituencies — conservatives, socialists, and far-leftists.

The two remaining tickets posed more of a threat. The "Greek Challenge" candidates stood to drain my party of badly needed sorority and fraternity votes. The other ticket, also with wide appeal to mainstream voters, featured an intelligent and articulate woman whose positions threatened to divide female supporters.

At a big school like UM, most candidates use bulletin boards as one of their best publicity tools across campus.

The campaign would be trying emotionally, financially, and physically. The first ticket to announce candidacy did so two months before election in late March. At UM, there is no formal campaign "period" — candidates can announce as early as they want and can campaign at anytime they want.

Further, I was the underdog candidate. I was the youngest presidential contender and had a relatively modest budget of about $1,500, compared to the front-runner's war chest of $3,500. Campaign spending can get out of hand here, which is why next year's elections will have a spending cap for the first time. I don't think MSA candidates should be buzzing the football stadium with planes pulling campaign banners.

Finally, I knew that I would have to work hard to balance the demands of schoolwork with constant campaigning. I currently maintain a high GPA and my grades actually went up during my year in office. With little free time, I was forced to plan out time for studying, and to take that time seriously. I was very conscientious about attending all classes until the days of election, then I focused on campaigning. Always, though, my first priority is my education.

Fortunately, the three previous presidents were members of my party, The Michigan Party, so I talked with my predecessors to find out what had worked for them. They reaffirmed what I already knew to be important: name recognition, message, and tenacity. They also drilled into me one point: focus on campus, not on student government. All too often, candidates become so entangled in internal debates about parliamentary procedure and grievances that they forget to appeal to the vast majority of students who have no connection whatsoever to student government. My running mate and I constantly checked ourselves to make sure we were directing our message to "Every Student."

Develop a message. Hence, when it came time to put a strategy together, I cast aside the losing tactics of my vice presidential campaign, and turned to three "F" words: friends, freshmen, and Fiona.

I found friends in all groups in which I was active, and so I reminded colleagues in classes, in my dormitory, and at the cafe where I worked to vote for me. These friends also comprised a cadre of campaign "worker bees" — those helpful in postering, distributing hand bills, and scheduling. Further, friends provided an invaluable source of financial support. At the time, MSA did nothing to limit campaign spending, so to stay competitive in a presidential race, candidates need a budget of at least $1,500 for posters, handbills, newspaper advertisements, and other publicity items. While my running mate and I provided the bulk of our budget with our own funds, we also were blessed with generous friends who donated $50 here and there to our campaign.

Freshmen are a godsend. Energetic and passionate, they are hard workers, often devoting themselves to such disagreeable tasks as outdoor postering, get-out-the-vote telephoning, and old-fashioned door-to-door campaigning. Since many freshmen have not been in college long enough to commit themselves to numerous other student groups, they tend to have more time to devote to student government — and to campaigns.

As if this weren't blessing enough, the fact that the University of Michigan houses some 9,500 freshmen in 10 residence halls — all with polling places — makes for an astounding voting bloc. I contacted each of my dorm-dwelling pals, asking for a "Ten Friends" party. Essentially, this meant going to that friend's room, meeting 10 of his or her friends on that hall, and asking each of the 10, in turn, to ask 10 people to vote for me. This allowed me to solicit votes more effectively; people tend to vote based on personality and actual encounters, as opposed to abstract propaganda. In my experience, it's much more rewarding, personally and electorally, to spend all evening in one dorm cafeteria with 400 freshmen than it is to give five-minute stump speeches in ten different fraternities. Freshmen are loyal, tenacious, AND THEY VOTE.

Going in, we had analyzed voting trends from previous elections. We knew how many votes it would take to win and had broken it down by resident halls. We knew where the most votes came from and focused our resources there.

Finally, I focused on me. One of the advantages to having an unusual name is that it's easily distinguishable from the more popular monikers. I played all sorts of games with "Fiona Rose," of which the most memorable is the following poster slogan: "At the University of Michigan, Roses are Blue." This phrase is mnemonically effective, as it ties in my name and the school's color with a popular poem fragment. To this day, two years after I first used the now-trite slogan, I still encounter people who know me only as that "Roses-Are-Blue Girl."

Be creative with your flyers. Postering in and of itself is hardly new, so I needed to be creative with my name AND with the media. Thus, I discarded the old practice of using 8 1/2" x 11" signs and brought in a new practice. I used half-sheets (8 1/2" x 5 1/2") with large lettering and few words. Whereas campaigners traditionally used black lettering on neon paper, with tedious bullet points outlining their committee experience, I used black text on plain white paper with no more than 10 words per half-sheet. Sometimes, in fact, the little posters said only one word: Rose. One constant throughout the series of posters was the phrase "Moving Forward..." designed so that the viewer would associate my ticket with progressive ideas and effective leadership. These signs were highly visible among the sea of competitors' propaganda and greatly figured in my name-recognition strategy.

In putting up all those posters, I relied on friends and freshmen for help. Since UM's dormitories have strict rules prohibiting most postering techniques, I asked friends to put one of my campaign posters on the outside of their room doors. This way, every passer-by saw my name, and no rules were violated. Also, with some 18 classroom buildings at UM and with fastidious custodians tearing down misplaced campaign posters EVERY night, I had to be ruthless in putting up a new batch each morning. I organized my campaign volunteers into teams of two and asked them to sign up for 7 a.m. poster runs on various mornings. With no limits on campaign length, postering stretched on for two weeks — a formidable undertaking for a candidate without volunteer help.

We employed other publicity techniques as well, inventing some new ones and improving older ones. A union print shop in Detroit supplied us with cheap lawn signs, which we placed along the busiest campus sidewalks. This same shop provided another campaign gadget: candies encased in "Vote Rose/Mehta" wrappers. These worked well, since student voters didn't toss them aside as they did handbills, and my ticket stood a better chance of being remembered for such a creative tactic.

My opponents, on the other hand, pared a large portion of their publicity money into three banners, which they intended to string up in key locations. But the banner was stolen, and a second was not hung in a visible spot. My opponents also didn't stretch to think of creative things. For example, using lawn signs is not a new campaign tactic, but it had never been done here before we did it. I will give credit to our opponents for handing out homemade cherry pies on election day (their vice presidential candidate's family owns a bakery). They had hoped this would translate into a full ballot box, but it instead meant full stomachs for our campaign workers.

Don't run on your popularity. It was important to me that my presidential campaign not devolve into a popularity contest. As such, focusing on getting out my name meant more than having people simply recognize "Fiona": it meant having people recognize what Fiona stands for.

For example, early on in my student government career, I became concerned with the welfare of the non-traditional students on campus. The demographic picture of higher education has changed substantially in the last decade, with more women, minorities, and returning students going to school than ever before. We estimated that about eight percent of our students were parents themselves, plus about 25 percent of our student body is non-white. Not enough has been done to meet these students' needs with respect to special services and cost burdens.

In particular, I devoted much time to advocating student-parents' needs. Many graduate and undergraduate students at the University of Michigan have children, but few can afford to pay for full-time, licensed child care. Often, child care surpasses tuition in cost. With this in mind, I worked with graduate-student groups, women's groups, and a single-parent network to assess what could be done. By the election, I had successfully placed a referendum item on the ballot, seeking a $1-per-student, per-term raise in the student fee to help defray students' child-care costs. The issue sparked much discussion among the student body and was covered assiduously by the campus newspaper.

Focus on broader issues. There's an important lesson to learn here. Such campuswide efforts should be the modus operandi for student leaders, because leadership entails bringing disparate groups to work together effectively. Furthermore, the publicity that such an endeavor generates is helpful in an election, as it points to the candi-date's commitment and abilities.

Thus, my message to the voters was as students at a public university, we can and should expect our school to do more in the way of assisting our non-traditional peers. This goal can be achieved through intergroup coordination, effective Assembly leadership, and responsible

Vice President Probir Mehta (left) and Rose celebrate their spring 1996 victory.

representation to the university administration.

The message having been established, I turned my attention to the actual running of the campaign. The campaign chair took on the job of scheduling speaking appearances at various campus group meetings. I usually went with a couple of candidates who had ties with a group — we had to do advance work since I would never go in cold. If you do, you possibly face an antagonistic crowd. My VP and I hit about 150 groups total — there are about 600 on campus. A couple of the groups endorsed us formally, and we added this to the bottom of our flyers. But most groups realize that no matter who wins, they still have to go up for funding, so it's better to remain officially impartial.

We then focused on the two presidential and one vice presidential debates. Usually around 20 people attend, but this year, 125 people showed up. Even with this larger turnout, I knew that the real audience was the media. Sure enough, the debates were scrutinized by *The Michigan Daily*, as well as on campus radio and TV. My preparation paid off, because my knowledge of university issues was obvious to the reporters, and I got good press hits throughout the rest of the campaign. The post-debate press was favorable — they asked questions about tuition, and it was clear I was the only one who had done research. Since the debate was sponsored by the engineering club, I had done some research about the special needs of engineering students, so I was able to address their concerns in detail.

Such good press continued due to the talents of our media coordinator who sent out press releases, prepared the platform packet, and designed posters. He made certain that we received plenty of coverage and monitored the "Letters to the Editor" page to make sure that we were not out-written. In one memorable stunt, he got the editors to print a letter penned by my 12-year-old brother, who wrote to protest an unflattering letter on my behalf. My brother's letter won much attention and certainly helped to show me as being more than just a student politician.

Lastly, the party chair coordinated party meetings and checked up on the other candidates on our slate — supporting them and briefing them on our latest press releases. He was a true morale booster and kept us focused on campaigning even when the headlines were negative and spirits were low.

Delegating responsibilities allowed my running mate and me to attend events and meet voters. We had a good assessment of which factions of the student body vote the heaviest: freshmen and Greeks. Neither my running mate nor I is Greek, but we recruited Greek candidates for our Party's slate and took them along as a sign of solidarity when we attended chapter meetings. These Greek connections came in handy on the two voting days of the election. Several fraternity houses required their pledges to hand out "Vote Rose" publicity to students around campus.

Go all out on election day. When it came down to the crucial voting days, we pulled out all the stops and prayed for warm weather. I positioned friends and fellow party candidates to hand out literature and campaign candy outside voting tables. My running mate and I, each having become highly recognizable through the campus newspaper's coverage, talked with as many voters as possible. The key is to make eye contact with each potential supporter, speak sincerely, shake his hand, and get out of his way so he can go vote for you.

After four bruising weeks of campaigning, I found myself handing out literature at the last open polling place, the Graduate Library, on the last night of voting. I was giving it my all until the very end. This time, unlike my first ill-advised campaign as a freshman, I had a much better feeling about my prospects: my ticket had established a clear, positive message, and we succeeded in making it heard. The headline in the next morning's paper — "Rose, Mehta to lead MSA" — confirmed this. We won with 1,300 votes to the second-place ticket's 800 votes, with some 15 percent of the 36,000 students. At UM we don't have run-offs, so the candidates with the most votes automatically win.

To anyone seeking the position of student body president, I offer this counsel: ask yourself why you belong in office, what you will do with the position, and how you are different from the other contenders. It's an arduous climb to the top, but with delegation, superior communication skills, and supporters, the climb is rewarding.

Contact: Fiona Rose
Address: 2718 Hampshire Road, Ann Arbor, MI 48104
E-mail: frose@umich.edu

From No Seat to the Best Seat At the University of Nebraska

By Jason Winterboer
1996-97 Student Government Association President
University of Nebraska at Omaha

Introduction

In addition to his SGA presidential duties, Winterboer works part-time at a local store and is preparing to take the LSAT.

After graduating with a degree in December 1997 in small business management, he plans to practice law or work in business.

How Winterboer Blanketed Campus to Win

I knew early on that my ultimate goal at college was to be president. And as I gained more experience in other campus activities, I knew I could be an effective one. In the University of Nebraska system, the student president also serves on the Board of Regents, the University's highest governing body. While I had absolutely no experience in student government, I always kept up-to-date on student senate business.

Before the elections, I learned as much as I possibly could about how SG operated, including exactly how the senate allocated student fees. As an outsider, I even attended senate and Board of Regents meetings, which helped me explain to voters and supporters what I actually would do if I won. It also was a great way to break the ice with unfamiliar groups and individuals.

Getting started. At UNO, when senators are removed or resign, vacant positions can be filled via appointment. I had applied for an open seat three times as a freshman and sophomore, but was rejected. After the last denial, I decided to go after the biggest seat instead.

I became heavily involved in other campus activities, surrounding myself with the best and most outgoing students on campus. Besides my involvement in the Greek community, I became president of UNO's union programming board, led new student orientation sessions during the summer, and worked on the honors program student advisory board. The connections to prominent student leaders in these organizations helped me tremendously during the elections. Not only were these leaders a solid voter base, but they proved to be among my most serious campaign volunteers.

I started early on my campaign, deciding to run in January 1996. In May 1996, I began by identifying key groups on the campus. UNO is a completely commuter campus, which usually means more apathy, and that makes the power of unified student groups substantial, as they seem to be the majority of the voter population. The obvious groups are the Greek system, athletic teams, and the special-interest groups, such as honor societies, the programming board, and minority interest groups, who meet regularly in the student center. We also wanted to appeal to less frequently noticed groups such as international students. They may not have been as visible as some other organizations on campus, but they did participate in many activities together and even made up a majority of students living in apartment buildings off-campus.

My three opponents came from many of these powerful, close-knit groups. One was a former football player, so he obviously knew many athletes. My other opponent was a five-year SG guru. I was Greek. With the main constituency groups largely represented, I had to market myself in a unique way to appeal to more than just Greeks.

I needed to draw on my diverse experience and leadership in different organizations. And while I wasn't an SG insider or a varsity letterman, I did have more than 1,500 hours invested in past leadership positions and activities. I talked about this record of service in every debate and newspaper ad.

We don't have running mates, so we promote only ourselves. While "selling" myself to the football team, I reminded the players that my fraternity was the one which brought a special cannon which fired at most home games. I reminded other groups of progress I had made on multi-cultural awareness, philanthropy, and monetary responsibility for the programming board. I had been a major contributor to the first annual Black History Month Museum, and to the first "Clothesline Across Campus" clothing drive. I also had agreed to permit a budget cut when the union programming board was up for review, a responsible move since UNO's board is entirely funded by student fees.

The stream of ads. Once you've announced your candidacy, be the first to use every form of advertising possible and try to make indelible memories in your voters' minds. That's easier said than done, I realize.

So I did something no one had ever done: I invited 120 friends and acquaintances to my home for a reception "announcing the president/regent candidacy of Mr. Jason L. Winterboer." Forty students attended and I gave my first campaign speech. News quickly spread about this announcement party, and everyone could see that I was a serious candidate.

Next, I developed attractive handbills and 11" x 17" posters that were done 45 days before election. I had my picture taken by a professional photographer, then took it to a friend who created ads for his student paper at another local university. He then helped write and design my poster.

Once the large sign was finished, I had it reduced to handbill size. Instead of including my entire resume, I included only my most notable leadership positions to avoid confusing the voters. As soon as the official election period started, with the help of volunteers, I personally posted the flyers on bulletin boards in all buildings. If you do it during the day, it can be great exposure, as professors and students will stop and talk with you about your candidacy.

I had 1,000 stickers printed, which were put on shirts, jackets, and book bags beginning at my campaign reception. By getting the stickers out early, I showed I was a serious and organized candidate. The other two candidates followed my lead. I was also sure to ration the number of stickers I used each day, as I wanted to be sure I had enough to give out during the election days and enough for campaign reps to wear while they distributed handbills by the polls.

Stickers may not work at your school, so decide which ad venues are best for your campus. At the UNO student center, large banner spaces in public areas, smaller free-standing sign holders, and table tents on cafeteria tables were absolutely a must. Candidates had to reserve the space through a supporting organization — I used my fraternity. The only time I wasn't first to use an advertising media was when I didn't reserve the cafeteria table space. One of my opponents found out and took advantage of my lapse. Later, many people asked me "Why aren't your ads on the table." Fortunately, at 8 a.m. the day after the first election, I reserved the table space for use during the second election campaign.

I definitely don't suggest spending precious advertising dollars for ads in your school newspaper, assuming that the paper covers the elections. During our primary campaign, every issue of the student paper had an article or editorial giving constant information on the qualifications, actions, and comments of the candidates. Using any money for paid ads definitely would have been a waste of money, since our paper wrote about the elections in detail in every issue. Placing ads, I think, would have been redundant, plus we had a very limited budget anyway. We're only allowed to spent $200 during the campaign, which is what we spent. I used my own money.

Speak anytime you can. You might not think of speeches as "advertising," but they're probably one of the most personal and effective "ads" your campaign can possibly have. Visit as many fraternities, sororities, special-interest organizations, honor societies, athletic teams, and even classes with the professors' permission, of course. To be courteous and respectful, communicate with each group's president, coach, or other key contact before

68

Immediately after he was named 1996-97 president, Winterboer celebrates his runoff election victory with friends and supporters. Photo by Chad Greene.

you arrive. Don't just show up unannounced or unexpected. One organization leader told me that one of my opponents was too pushy, and she reported this obtrusiveness to the campus paper.

I started making appointments 30 days before the election, the earliest I could legally make such contacts. While speaking, stay brief and leave time to field questions. Don't overstay your welcome — it's OK to be a little shorter than you expected, but definitely don't go over your allotted time. Another opponent gave several speeches lasting nearly 20 to 30 minutes, which were perceived as awfully long and inconsiderate to the groups.

Lastly, distribute your handbills to meeting participants so they will remember you. Some close-knit groups have discussions about who they'll vote for and often vote for the same candidate.

Closely related to speeches are the infamous debates. Whether the debate is staged by Student Government, campus organizations, or the campaign managers, stay clear of attacking a candidate's personality or becoming visibly upset at an opponent's comments. You want to be viewed as level-headed, smooth, and relaxed. Believe me, the press will pick up on these attributes and favor you for not appearing brash or irrational. Whether it's in debates or speeches, be prepared to answer absolutely any question, stupid or intelligent. I was asked everything from why beer wasn't served on our dry campus to why more bachelor's degree programs weren't offered. Don't be afraid to admit that you do not know the answer to a question — say you'll research the answer and respond at a later date. The debates weren't well-attended — about 100 people showed up at the first one. The second event attracted only about 15 students who admittedly were mainly my supporters. I'm not sure that I got new voters as a result of the debates, but lots of students came up to me afterward and said they were supporting me. The debates did get covered by the paper.

People like to be rewarded for their graciousness. Send follow-up thank you cards to the organizations who gave you time. Thank them sincerely for letting you speak, and offer to answer any other questions they may have.

One last advertising tip: have your friends do mass e-mailings to as many or all students on campus, if it's permitted. You might be surprised at how many people addictively read their e-mail, especially from an unknown sender.

Through all of your ads and public appearances, try to create distinct memories in your voters' minds. Create ads and publicity about yourself which are unique and creative, but not absurd or repulsive. Your actions will at times speak louder than the words leaving your lips. For example, during the debate sponsored by the student newspaper, all candidates were given a few minutes to make a closing statement. While my other two opponents gave good closing remarks, they delivered them from the podium. I decided to stand up, leave the stage, and deliver my closing statement from the middle of the audience. To this day, the editor of our paper can't believe I did this during the debate. A photograph of me leaving the stage ended up on the front page of the paper. It took people off guard, and I think they were impressed that I showed that much enthusiasm.

Dealing with controversy. This year's elections brought up a maelstrom of controversy. From allegations of sexual harassment and misconduct to anonymous letters supposedly from other presidential candidates stating they would file campaign grievances against other candidates, the press certainly aired any and all controversy surrounding the candidates. While I was questioned frequently, I always stated my preference not to comment on the these superfluous issues I felt were irrelevant to the campaign. I instead stressed why I was qualified for office and what I wanted to do for the student body.

If competitors attack your character or past activities, again disregard these remarks as a sign of immaturity and consider their actions an indication that they're self-conscious about the substance of their own qualifications or experience.

Be ready for change, quick change! You'll find that opinions change by the hour and tactics your competitors use multiply by the minute.

Be prepared to change your printed materials when necessary — keep them safely on a computer disk so changes can be made easily. For example, after the primary election, I decided to add the facts about the 1,500 hours of service I had given to campus organizations to my flyers and posters.

Usually, all candidates campaign just outside or inside the student center; we aren't allowed to get any closer than 30 feet from the polls. One of my opponents set up a chair and large sign then began shouting as people passed him, "Vote for me, I'm not a politician." That day I knew I had to focus even more on my experience. Individually, I spoke to students and they generally listened attentively to my low-key, mini "speeches" about my campus contributions.

If multiple candidates are in the race, there may be a run-off election. And candidates who ran against you during the primary election could prove to be your greatest supporters during the run-off election. So maintain positive relations with the other candidates and always be a "good sport." While this may be hard

at first, never respond or act mean-spirited to your competitors. Instead, try complimenting them on a well-done speech or poster. I used the friendly approach early on in my campaign. One of my opponents definitely was a political enemy before the elections started, so I went and spoke to her and addressed some general questions about the elections. Amazingly, we actually became friends during the election and discovered that we drew support from many of the same people, which probably hurt both campaigns and perhaps forced the run-off.

The other opponent and I had started off on a friendly note but unfortunately didn't end on the best of terms. I guess we probably disagreed about each other's qualifications, and we ended up being the two biggest competitors. So everything we did was to combat the other's strategies, and that created some hard feelings. Plus, after the primary was over and a run-off election was announced, the candidate I had befriended publicly endorsed me in the student paper, *The Gateway*, which is published bi-weekly. This absolutely helped me win the election, as many of her voters supported me. A lot of her supporters told me that they were going to back me and they started wearing our stickers and passing out flyers.

I changed my physical appearance, much to the surprise of some of my volunteers. I usually wore a tie to all speeches I made and wore a suit on both election days during the first election. During the second campaign, however, I shed the formal attire and wore jeans and a sweatshirt. I changed because after the first election, I heard some feedback that people did not think that I looked like a "regular student" — I was too dressed up. This situation might not apply at your campus, so get a feeling for what students expect their student leaders to look like. Please note, however, I did wear khaki pants and a nice shirt when I spoke to organizations. I was gradual in making this change. It wasn't one day in a suit, then the next in shredded jeans.

During the run-off, I felt I wasn't reaching an enormous, united group of students: the international students. I was dropping off flyers at their off-campus residences, but I knew I needed more. With the help of my assistant campaign manager, we put "Vote Jason Winterboer for Student President" on the backs of my handbills in three other languages: Farsi, Japanese, and Chinese, which are large populations. We also utilized two, 24" x 36" standing signs which could be reserved from the student center. This was extremely effective — I saw scores of international students stopping to read the signs. The multilingual messages were on the backs of my handbills which had a miniature version of my posters on the front. When international students walked by (and we were certain they were in the international program) we flipped the flyer over and handed it to them with the multilingual messages showing. One piece of advice, though, is to make sure the characters and spelling of foreign languages are correct. One slight jerk of the hand can completely change the meaning behind a character in Chinese, for example.

Be ready to change and replace friends and volunteers you might be relying on. In essence, don't trust anyone except your core of trusted confidantes. Only three or four people knew my really detailed strategies. Watch what you say to people you don't know well. There were people who I thought supported me who didn't, and I didn't find this out until later. You can't know the hidden political agendas of every person on your campus. I had campaign volunteers leak secret information and assist opponents for very self-motivated reasons. Always watch what you say about others, too. It's relatively easy for people to twist comments as they become second- and third-hand renditions of what you had said.

Be prepared to react, or in some cases not react, to the seemingly bizarre actions of your competitors. I had one competitor tape me while I gave a speech to his organization. This took me by surprise because in the three years of being active on campus, I had never seen or heard of a student presidential candidate tape recording a speech. I don't know what he hoped to accomplish, but he was probably analyzing it, as his platform wasn't as well-shaped as mine.

Election day. Two weeks before the election, begin scheduling volunteers to help hand out flyers at the polls every hour the polls are open. You personally should plan to be at the polls every minute too. The only time I left was to go to the restroom. Ask friends and colleagues to sign up for an hour or two on a master volunteer schedule. Make sure you have more people scheduled in the mornings, noon hour, and any other extremely busy time. The night before the election, call everyone who signed up and thank them for volunteering, also reminding them of when they had signed up. Once the election is over, remember to thank these people. Lastly, keep in contact with those students who helped you, especially if you know there will be a run-off election and you may need their assistance again.

I attribute much of my victory to dedicated friends and colleagues. They handed out my literature and gave me tremendous moral support. One reason I won was I always had at least three students giving out handbills by the polls at all times. This sent a clear message to my opponents that I was a serious contender. While they were struggling to meet voters, I was doing it with ease thanks to my volunteers. In fact, one candidate called my volunteers "mice", which to me was a clear indication that their presence was irritating and damaging to my opponent's moral.

Campaigning near the polls both inside and outside of the polling place is a great way, especially on our commuter campus, to catch nontraditional students and non-involved students as they walk to class. This technique was very important here, because the average age of our students is 27 years old, and they're typically not as involved.

Voters passing by will ask questions ranging from beer sales to bachelor degrees. Be mentally prepared to answer all types of questions. Don't be afraid to spend too much time talking to one person and fear "losing" other votes. This situation is one which was greatly alleviated by having a full force of election day volunteers to pass out handbills. As I was answering questions or campaigning, my cohorts were after other voters.

At the end of your election, throw a party at a local restaurant or bar. Invite friends, colleagues, and definitely the people who helped you on your campaign. If your school newspaper is anything like ours, they'll come when the election commission announces its results. Be prepared with statements, if you win or lose. Also, give thanks to those who helped you on your campaign and voted for you. Everybody likes praise.

One last election day tip: finish all your homework early, attend class up until elections, and get adequate sleep, particularly the night before your election. I know I sound like your mother, but you'll be much more relaxed if you have taken care of academic duties, and your professors will respect you for going to class. I admit that I definitely missed some classes, but my grades only decreased slightly from a 3.84 GPA to a 3.81, which concerned me. I spent about 35 hours a week campaigning. But I'm not sure that time spent campaigning led to this small drop — I just had a couple really tough classes related to my major.

Also, don't forget to eat — I'm serious. You'll be so busy and stressed that you may actually forget.

What if you have a run off? Take a break, even if it's short — but only after you take care of any pressing strategic planning for your second campaign. For example, I had to reserve all student union advertising space at 8 a.m. on the day following the first election or lose precious exposure. Give yourself some time to relax, enjoy hobbies, catch up on school work, and touch base with your friends. This is very important to maintain your sanity. Remember, too much of any one thing is bad. If you reach this point, you'll probably feel that campaign work has become excessive.

Your previous banners may be out of date, in disrepair, or destroyed by any number of means. A marble floor requires repolishing to show its strength and beauty, and you'll need to "repolish" your ads.

Speak to more student organizations, but this time tone down your speech and give only the most pertinent reasons of why you're the best candidate for the position. By doing this, you'll be showing respect for the organization's time and busy agenda, and exhibiting an assumption that the organization members are intelligent human beings capable of remembering your previous speeches. Also, by this time, the campus media has probably had the elections and your quotes and platform splashed all over its pages for some time. Students have probably seen at least some of them.

Don't ever give up. Don't ever think for even a second that you won't win. Every action you take and word you speak should be performed with utmost confidence. I'm not suggesting that you be arrogant. Just do the best you can under your prevailing conditions and resources. My campaign manager, volunteers, and consultants would never, ever discuss losing, except when I prepared my comments regarding a possible win or loss for when the newspaper interviewed me.

When the results were finally announced, I had 495 votes to 318 for my opponent. During the first election, I had 450, while my opponents got 410 and 250 votes respectively. The voter turnout was higher than normal, probably because of all the press coverage and because we have a brand new student center, so students are staying on campus more. Plus, all of the candidates worked hard to get voters involved.

Good luck. During your campaign, you'll learn a great deal about those who know and support you. You'll discover your work habits, good or bad, and how every action you take is responded to by the student body. Win or lose, you'll have learned the discipline it takes to pursue something you have always dreamed of having. In my case I gained a wonderful student career, not to mention a fiancee. Soon after the elections, I became engaged to my lovely campaign manager, Javine Horani. Her love and hard work on the campaign pushed me through the toughest of times.

Contact: Jason Winterboer
Address: 3110 S. 162nd Circle, Omaha, NE 68130
Phone: (402) 334-7631
Fax: (402) 554-2583 (SGA office)
E-mail: jwinterb@s-cwis.unomaha.edu

An Underdog Independent Wins At North Carolina State University

By John O'Quinn
1995-96 Student Government President
North Carolina State University

Introduction

O'Quinn, 22, was valedictorian of his graduating class, was elected to Phi Beta Kappa, and was a John T. Caldwell Alumni Scholar at NC State. He graduated with degrees in chemical engineering and multidisciplinary studies.

He currently is a Fulbright Scholar pursuing a master's degree in environmental management at Oxford University in England.

How O'Quinn Won as a Non-Greek Candidate

I wrote in my campaign platform "A Student Body President must not only serve as the chief advocate for students, but also provide a vision for students, faculty, and administrators — the University as a whole. My vision is simple: We must take pride in our heritage and plan efficiently for the future. Students from around the state, nation, and globe invest their futures at NC State University. They have a right to certain expectations. Making sure these are met is what my presidency will be about." My campaign platform obviously set some idealistic goals, but no matter how noble any leader's aspirations may be, they're for naught unless he or she can get elected.

Prior to running for office, I served in the Student Senate. I watched many presidential elections, and personally knew the students who were my immediate predecessors. The campaign advice they gave me was the keystone to their elections and my victory — "You must know the numbers."

As a freshman among 27,000 students, I remember wondering how anyone could possibly put together a campaign for the highest office on campus. I had been casually involved in my high school student council and was elected to the Senate as a college freshman, but both of those roles seemed like peanuts compared to the student body presidency.

To make it even harder, we had a spending limit of $125 in the general election and $50 for a runoff. This limit was monitored by an Elections Board to which candidates reported supplies and expenditures — even in-kind donations had to be given a dollar value. Furthermore, active campaigning was restricted to two weeks prior to the general election.

Find out how many votes you need to win. I soon realized that only a fraction of our students vote. In fact, the average turnout is less than 10 percent, not unusual for a large public university, meaning 1,000 votes can usually spell victory. In recent years, the numbers had been even smaller. Identifying the 2,700 or so that would be most likely to vote was the key to winning an election, and the best people to help me identify the voting students were my predecessors. I was fortunate to share a room during a Summer-in-Oxford program with Chris Jones, a two-term student body president (1992-94), and to benefit from his advice and experience.

On my campus, the major traditional voting blocks consist of fraternities and sororities, large minority groups, and, to a lesser extent, students living on-campus. The Greek system, I was told, has a history of dominating campus politics in the executive branch at NC State. It had been at least a decade since a non-Greek had been elected president.

I began planning my campaign over the 1994-95 Christmas break. I wasn't at all convinced that I could be elected, because I didn't have a network of Greek groups to mobilize. What I did have was a strong desire to serve and determination to run a good campaign.

Although I didn't know that the final field of candidates, set in early March 1995, would be five rising seniors, I did know that two of my opponents would be tough competition. One was a colleague in the Student Senate who was from a strong fraternity and the other was the senate president. My election was guaranteed to be an uphill battle.

Get your friends involved. Early on, starting in conversations with friends and expanding outward, I began building my coalition. My sister Emily, who was a freshman, has described my campaign as a true grass-roots effort. I didn't have a single "machine" to depend on. Instead, I had to develop strategies to mobilize parts of the student body that usually don't vote.

These ideas came from many sources, including local politicians, key friends in my campaign, and leaders of smaller campus organizations. I didn't have a campaign manager, so I organized and coordinated almost my entire election effort myself. I did have several "campaign chiefs," including my sister, whom I could count on to hang posters, speak to organizations, hand out flyers, and paint the "free expression tunnel" that connects two parts of our campus. Other "chiefs" included friends from my years in Student Government and InterVarsity Christian Fellowship, some of whom later served in my administration.

Many of these same students helped me craft my platform, a critical element in my success. Broad and comprehensive — perhaps too comprehensive in that it was criticized by the student newspaper, *The Technician*, as unachievable — my platform was the foundation not only for my speeches during the campaign, but for executive branch activities once I took office.

The issues I focused on throughout the campaign were: campus safety (still a hotly debated issue), facilities improvement, changes in academic policy, and affordable tuition.

Because I got input from a broad range of peers, I was able to choose issues that affected the overwhelming majority of the student body and were well-received, judging by some of the unsolicited letters of support written to the student newspaper. In picking my focus, I also looked at issues debated in previous elections, resolutions passed by the Student Senate, and concerns raised in recent newspaper articles and editorials. While the whole platform wasn't widely distributed, it was influential in attracting some of my early support, because it convinced students such as scholars, resident assistants, and fellow senators that I was a candidate with a serious agenda.

In building a coalition, my goal was to achieve "the magic number" of votes to get elected — and then try to triple or quadruple it. Not everyone you think will vote for you will, or will even remember to go to the polls.

I took full advantage of being the only engineering major running for president, and hoped to count on lots of support from the College of Engineering, which makes up almost a third of the student body. Our college was facing administrative cuts — an issue I campaigned against — so I got a great deal of support from the Student Engineers Council, professional societies, and my academic department, Chemical Engineering. Many of my former professors invited me into their classrooms to talk to students.

I had been involved with InterVarsity Christian Fellowship since my freshman year and am still grateful to InterVarsity and other christian fellowships, such as New Generation Ministries and Fellowship of Christian Athletes, for their tremendous support. Many of my campaign workers were InterVarsity members, while others were peers from Student Government.

In addition to engineering professors, I asked friends among the faculty for a few minutes at the beginning of their larger classes. This gave me opportunities to speak to 200 or more students at a time, particularly freshmen.

Using phone lists available from the Office of Student Development, I also contacted the presidents of student organizations to see if I could speak to their groups. During the two weeks of permissable campaigning and the runoff, my campaign chiefs and I spoke to nearly 50 organizations.

I asked other RAs in my building to encourage their residents to vote — our building alone could potentially yield almost 1,000 votes.

I even had a strategy for hanging posters. Although candi-

To get publicity, O'Quinn and his staff painted a campaign sign in the "Free Expression Tunnel" that connects two parts of North Carolina State's campus.

dates were required to hang their own 8 1/2" x 11" posters at least three feet apart, I hung my posters side by side with my sister's, who was running for reelection to the Senate. Her posters read "O'QUINN" in big letters, with "Emily, that is — for Student Senate" in smaller print underneath. Thus I had double exposure. (Emily went on to receive the largest number of votes of any candidate for any Senate seat, so the exposure helped her too!)

One of my unique strategies focused on opposing a threatened tuition increase from the NC General Assembly. Having a large population of students working part-time, our campus would be severely affected by any tuition increase. Friends in the College Republicans chapter volunteered to staff a campus booth to collect signatures on a petition opposing the tuition increase. We then presented this petition to legislators. Not only was this event covered in the campus paper, but I was able to set up a local phone bank to call the students who signed the petition, thanking them for opposing a tuition increase and asking them to vote for John O'Quinn in the upcoming election.

A final unique strategy was having a running mate. While this is quite common on many campuses, NC State doesn't have a student body vice president. Instead, the student senate president, elected by the student body, is the de facto vice president. These two people are elected independently, don't necessarily collaborate, and for that matter, don't even have to like each other.

I asked a former suite mate, Robert Zimmer, who was serving in the Senate, to run for Senate President and to be my running mate. After discussing strategy, he agreed. Robert was an asset on the campaign trail, because we could cover more ground independently and when together present a united front. In addition, he and I were able to work closely together after we were elected. Although Robert won his race in the general election, my candidacy drug out into a run-off, and he continued to help me campaign. I'm pleased to add that in the 1996 elections, he succeeded me as president.

Don't count on good press. Unfortunately, or fortunately as it turned out, no election goes exactly as planned. At a large school like ours, it's almost impossible to account for the media and the mudslinging that newspapers tend to provoke. I did plan a few media strategies, such as presenting the petition to the General Assembly and soliciting letters of endorsement in *The Technician*, including a strong letter from a state representative with whom I had worked in the past.

What I didn't anticipate was being the subject of negative news stories. One article reported that "John O'Quinn could be disqualified from the race because of e-mail campaign rule violations." A student who was not part of my campaign had sent an e-mail message to a listserver recommending that students talk to me to find out if I represented their interests. Using the newspaper as a forum, one of my opponents argued that I should be disqualified, claiming that one of my supporters had violated an election rule that banned the use of university equipment, including computer systems, in campaigning. While this argument was rejected by the Elections Board, the publicity raised awareness of my campaign to the average student.

Later, my use of phone calls encouraging students to vote roused more controversy. One of my opponents said the phone calls violated campaign rules, because they were not an "approved" campaign method — a ridiculous assertion since phones are commonly used in most state and local campaigns, and had been used at NC State in the past. The Elections Board again ruled that I was still eligible, although they did issue me a warning for not first having cleared it with them.

Although this negative publicity was disconcerting, even heartbreaking at the time, it turned out to be one of the best things that could have happened. Not only was my name on the front page of nearly every edition of our tri-weekly campus newspaper, but the attacks galvanized my supporters, who were convinced that the media, which had endorsed an opponent, was out to get me. Casual friends in my classes became staunch supporters overnight, and students who had never voted decided to participate in the election. I know this because so many students came up to me after class and said something to the effect of, "John, I've never voted on campus before, but I'm going to do it for you." Unsolicited letters of support appeared in the campus paper, including one that said one of my opponents was "merely attempting to rid herself of, arguably, the most qualified candidate to represent the student body."

After two intense weeks of campaigning, the general election ended with a total of 2,681 students voting — 1,000 more than had participated in the previous year's election. I got the most votes with 33 percent or 986 votes compared to 669 for my top challenger, which put us into a runoff election.

My remaining opponent had served in the Senate and had received many endorsements from the Greek community as well as the support of parts of the African American community. The runoff was very close in my favor, 994 to 916. Despite my apparent victory with 52 percent of the vote, my opponent appealed the final tally. He said that fewer polling places were provided in the runoff election, so the results should be invalidated and new elections held. Before finally being declared president-elect, I had to demonstrate to a student review board that this was true of runoffs in previous elections and had no bearing on the fairness of the election or on the outcome.

In retrospect, my election was a lot of fun, in spite of losing 10 pounds and remaining under constant stress and pressure during the three weeks of campaigning and the appeal. I had to skip lots of classes, so having understanding professors who were supportive and flexible was important. Several allowed me to postpone tests, which kept my grades from suffering. I maintained the 4.0 GPA. I had prior to the election not only through my campaign, but through my year in office as well. Although the election was important, academics were my top priority in college.

Serving as student body president was one of the most challenging and enriching experiences of my life. It was well worth the campaign trials. If my election proved anything, it is that with faith, hope, and hard work, anyone can be elected student body president. To this day I don't really know where I actually got all my support. I wasn't expected to win. I just know that through God's grace the support came in, one vote at a time.

Contact: John O'Quinn
Address: 8005 Kensington Drive,
Fuquay-Varina, NC 27526

A Techno Candidate Wins at Miami University of Ohio

By Tom Adams
1996-97 Associated Student Government President
Miami University, Ohio

Introduction

In addition to serving as president, Adams, 22, worked as a technology intern for ASG and was involved in the Delta Sigma Pi business fraternity and Mortar Board.

After graduating with a dual major in finance and accounting in May 1997, Adams took a trip to Europe before settling into work at a firm that deals with emerging technologies.

How Adams' High-Tech Campaign Won

I always knew I might someday run for ASG president. However, it wasn't until three weeks before the spring 1996 election that I finally came to terms with what I could offer my university and decided to go for it. Before that, I had no significant impetus to run, nor did I have a platform. If I had run before, it would have been as a candidate trying to maintain the status quo in a slightly better way than my opponents. That was a weak argument and didn't motivate me to make the effort. It certainly would not have captivated the student body like my platform and campaign did later.

While my campaign was a success because of a number of techniques, I won primarily because I had a sincere, timely, and well-communicated platform — a vision that was right for our student government at that time.

When I communicated this vision to my friends, they loved it and were motivated to help. And more importantly, when I told complete strangers, they actually listened. With my unique platform, I separated myself from the traditional candidates and beat the incumbent ASG executive vice president, who everyone thought was destined to win. I won handily in our primary, despite running against two opponents, which most of the time means a runoff. In my case, the platform was the most crucial element of my victory.

Choose issues students care about. So what was my vision? Simply put, I decided to run knowing that my technical experience could be an asset to ASG as Miami University moved toward an "electronic campus."

A few years earlier, the University had a made a commitment to install a data/video network in all residence hall rooms. This network would bring the Internet and cable TV to all 7,000 on-campus students. In addition, MU planned to provide dial-in lines to the 8,000 off-campus students so they could connect to the internet.

I had served on ASG in various non-officer roles as a freshman, sophomore, and junior. I also worked in the computer labs, first as a consultant and ultimately as a technician, so I had learned about different computing technologies, networking, and the Internet in particular. I became somewhat of a technical junkie in that I taught myself the ins and outs of most personal computers and even how to write programs on Miami's multi-user machines.

The focus on technology started to "click" almost immediately. I had conversations with friends and tried my pitch on them, describing how I saw Miami making major technological advances in the near future and the need for student involvement in the process. Since each student would be paying as much as $90 per semester for the network, the University needed to enable them to access this new technology. While it's easy to install the network connection in every room, the challenge is to provide the informational resources so students can use it.

I also wanted ASG to take advantage of the new technology by providing services such as a cable television channel guide and technology bulletin boards for every residence hall. I already had created a program to help students buy and sell textbooks electronically, and I wanted to move it to the web. I also wanted ASG to conduct on-line student opinion polls and help campus organizations and individual students learn how to make their own web home pages.

I wasn't sending mixed messages to the student body about what I intended to accomplish, because I wasn't trying to be everything to everyone. I was the "technology presidential candidate," and this approach worked.

Despite the importance of the platform, it was only the foundation of my campaign. The next task was to deliver the message to as many students as possible to spark their interest in voting. We had serious competition: the number-two person in ASG was well-connected and had experience. A third candidate ran on a religious platform, but was not expected to get many votes.

I had hoped for an endorsement from our twice-weekly campus newspaper, *The Miami Student*, but its editors expected a runoff and didn't make an endorsement during the primary. They also didn't write much about the upcoming elections, except to include several articles about my opponent. Another campus paper, *The Miami Forum*, actually named my competitor the "Most Influential Student on Campus," which made my candidacy seem all the more foolhardy.

Keep banners simple. Needless to say, we had to go all out with conventional campaigning just to keep up. But with a total permitted budget of $200, creativity was the key. The spending limit discourages political parties from forming, because a party "ticket" would have a total budget of $200 rather than $200 for each candidate. Fortunately, my mother is an artist and she created eye-catching, professional-looking banners. She used vinyl letters that she cut out and affixed to a sturdy, light-colored tarp. The message was simple: "Adams for President." The banner, along with all printed campaign materials, included my web site address: http://www.muohio.edu/~tgadams.

At Miami, the rules prevent official campaigning until 7:30

a.m. on the sixth day before the Tuesday election. It's first-come, first-served for prime sign space. We staked out one of the best banner locations above the hub in our academic quad about 12 hours earlier and hung a rolled-up dummy banner. The banner was blank and anyone could have taken it down, but it effectively held the spot because no one called our bluff and removed it. In the morning, we replaced the decoy.

We also had three other professional banners for which we found key locations in the academic quad, in a residential area, and near the student union. If your campus has quad residential living, spots where students will see your banner on the way to or from classes are invaluable.

On the first day of campaigning, I asked 20 friends to join me at 7 a.m. to load up with 8 1/2" x 11" flyers. We tied them to trees and stapled them back-to-back on chain link fences around campus. If they got torn down, we put them right back up. There really aren't any restrictions on where you can put signs, with two exceptions: signs were not permitted inside academic buildings and they cannot be stapled or tacked to trees. My signs didn't include any details about my platform, they just said "Adams for President." More than anything, we wanted students to at least remember my name if they decided to vote.

Don't forget the dorms. About a week before campaigning began, I developed a list of friends who lived in each of the 37 residence halls on campus. These students were given flyers and brochures and were asked to hang them on bulletin boards and in the bathrooms. Some of the signs were void of detailed information and were meant to make students laugh. Many people on campus couldn't care less about student government, the candidates, or the issues, and these signs were designed to get their attention.

One of the signs had a picture of *The Addams Family* from the old TV show. I superimposed my head on Pugly Addams' body. It was humorous and I heard afterwards that many people decided to vote for me solely because they liked my publicity. One of our most offbeat 8 1/2" x 11" signs included a picture of my dog

Adams

for

President

he comes from a background of
strong family values

for more information, please visit:
http://www.muohio.edu/~tgadams

with my head superimposed, and I strategically placed these signs on fire hydrants around campus.

I also made up a "Top 10" list on a flyer and placed copies in the stall of every dorm bathroom. This list was a mix of frivolity and substance. It took about two minutes to read the entire page, but we knew we had a captive audience, and many students enjoyed the humor. We also learned that election dates should be mentioned prominently on all publicity materials. It's one thing to foster people's interest, but if they don't know how and when to vote, potential votes are lost.

Get out and meet students. After we hung as many flyers as possible, it was time to "close the deal." I think the most effective campaigning is person-to-person. It's good for people to see your signs around campus, but it's much more powerful for people to meet the person behind the publicity. Nothing, and I mean nothing, beats the personal touch.

Sorority weekly group meetings are held on Wednesday night, and we went to six different suites six days before the election. Our presentation was a humorous skit that we created about 30 minutes before the first scheduled appearance. One of my best friends, a six-foot Russian named Natan, went with me. Dressed in suits, we entered the room and he introduced me as a candidate for president. My mouth was taped and he did all the talking. He told the audience about all of the lofty goals that I wanted to achieve, if elected. According to Natan, I wanted to personally ensure that everyone gets a job, 24-hour access to the dining halls, and a computer. While he explained these "promises," I rolled my eyes in disbelief and waved my arms. He concluded his dialogue in his Russian accent with "Isn't that right, Tom?" and ripped the tape off my mouth so I could say, "No way, what are you talking about?" I then apologized to the crowd, explaining that obviously those things weren't possible. I then comfortably segued into the real platform, highlighting specific planks like 24-hour computer lab access and on-line course registration.

It's important to leave a group with your most important and memorable issues. At the end, we asked for questions and left, often with a round of applause. We deliberately tried to be playful and still convey the sincere commitment that our campaign represented. Even if people weren't interested in technology, they perceived me to be truly interested in the job and in helping our school. Sometimes, that's all students need to see and they'll remember you.

We spent other evenings canvassing every residence hall room. Miami's policies delineate specific hours when this is allowed, 7 to 10 p.m., so we had to hurry. Usually, a team of three would split up, knock on doors, and say who they were representing. We handed residents a small handbill that had a picture of a compact disc titled "Adams for President." This faux CD featured 10 "songs" listing my past accomplishments as "current hits." If students had more questions, we would stick around or I would visit them personally.

During campaign week, we hit every freshman residence hall and even a few upperclass halls. The freshmen are emphasized in Miami elections for several key reasons. They are required to live on campus and tend to vote more readily. They also tend to be more interested and impressed by candidates running for office. It's all new to them and they usually look up to upperclass students.

I can't overemphasize the need to go out and meet people. In addition to the sororities, I also talked to my business fraternity and attended a hall government forum. Most of my talks were with individual students, however.

Try new ideas. Since we had the conventional campaign well-covered, it was time to be unconventional. A month before the election, I had discovered a completely legal way to collect the User I.D.s of every person who logged into one of our multi-user computers. I developed a program that ran every minute for a month in advance, collecting names as people logged in. I also discovered a way, using another program I wrote, to sort out the faculty, staff, and non-undergraduate students from that master list. This was important since only undergrads vote in our elections and I was conscious of not bothering too many other people. I wrote a third program that would send individual e-mail messages to each person on that filtered list. This gave each letter the appearance of being more personal than a message sent to everyone at the same time.

We wrote a letter that included my platform, experience, and

ADAMS
FOR
PRESIDENT

HTTP://WWW.MUOHIO.EDU/~TGADAMS

how to vote. Then, during eight hours on the first day of campaigning, we sent it to more than 5,000 students. Not long after, I started receiving responses from students. Not all of them were positive — about 20 percent were quite angry with me because I sent them "junk mail." The other 80 percent were impressed with being contacted in this way. I personally responded to everyone who wrote back to thank them or apologize. Surprisingly, some of the angry respondents softened after getting my follow-up letter. One person who was very harsh initially said something like "I was just trying to see if you would respond. I'm impressed — you've got my vote." Again, this proves how effective personal contact is, compared with other less interactive means of campaigning. Mass e-mailing had never been tried at our school, so it caught everyone by surprise, including my opponents. Now, mass e-mail messages aren't permitted during campaigns, but I had the benefit of being the first to try.

Get a web site. Our election year started a new tradition. Most campaigns now have a web page, but we were the first. Mine listed my experience, platform, and goals, along with some fun technology demos. I put a working demonstration of my book resale program on-line and created a "virtual student union" where people viewing the site could talk to each other. The web site was the most comprehensive information source for my campaign. I figured it would be visited by students who wanted to know more, so the web address was included on *all* publicity materials. The site looked great and even had excerpts from our campaign theme song: "Don't You Forget About Me [at the polling station]" by Simple Minds. The site received about 400 hits during campaign week.

Every campaign needs something different to grab attention. Conventional campaigning is necessary, but many students will tune it out. Two years before, candidate Mike Coffey put his name on a wooden coffee cup that said "Coffey for President" and placed it in front of the dining halls. People talked about that big cup for years. Techniques like this can give you extra mileage when you're trying to get a message out.

If you don't ask, you don't get. The final technique we used involved three uptown bars. My campaign manager, Shaun Schottmiller, and I personally went to a few establishments and asked them if they would be willing to use "Adams for President" ink stamps on their customers' hands. To our amazement, three said yes. One of them even offered a special shot called the

"Adams for President Shot." It was my father's recipe called "Moose-lips," and they allowed us to put up signs advertising the drink for a special price. They were so good to us that we brought in all of our friends after the election for the victory party.

After the polls closed at 10 p.m. on Tuesday night, my friends and I awaited the results. When they still weren't released by 2:30 a.m., everyone went home. We later learned that there had been some problems with the on-line voting mechanism that delayed the announcement. Finally, at 3 a.m., the outgoing student body president called and asked to meet with me. I thought there must be a problem but when I saw the champagne bottle she was holding, immediately I knew I had won. With a total voter turnout of about 15 percent, I captured about 1,300 votes or 55 percent, while my top opponent got 35 percent. The third place candidate finished with 10 percent. The total voter turnout was comparable with previous years but has since increased to about 25 percent, thanks to more accessible on-line voting.

My time as president provided me with many unique and beneficial experiences. Admittedly, I did sacrifice to be so involved and my grades suffered a little, but not because I didn't attend class. After devoting 20 to 30 hours a week to my ASG duties and projects, I just didn't have the time to study. I was able to graduate with a 3.0 GPA — lower than I had hoped, but I wouldn't trade my student government experience for anything.

I found out during the campaign that it doesn't matter how many people a candidate knows — if students don't know about the election or don't get out to vote, it doesn't matter. Every candidate has a window of opportunity to spread his or her message, and every candidate is beatable. The candidate with drive, creativity, and a solid vision will win.

Contact: Tom Adams
Address: 5830 Granby St., Worthington, OH 43085
E-Mail: adamstg@muohio.edu

The Four-Step Plan for Victory At Samford University

By Hunter Brewer
1996-97 Student Government Association President
Samford University, Alabama

Introduction

Brewer, 22, served on the Student Recruitment Team, was a member of Pi Kappa Phi fraternity, and was involved in Young Life, a Christian outreach group.

After graduating in May 1997 with a degree in public administration, Brewer is attending law school at the University of Alabama.

How Brewer Went From Prankster To President

Success doesn't just happen. You have to set everything in motion. This is an adage which, if investigated, would prove to be true of all Student Government presidents from Maine to California. In reality, being president is much like being the mayor of a small town. To tackle something this large, begin planning well in advance. When campaigning starts, a prepared candidate should be winding down his or her bid for the presidency.

I was elected president at Samford, a private university with an enrollment of 4,800, in the spring of 1996. I captured 71 percent of the vote with a turnout of 31 percent.

The wheels began turning soon after I was elected junior class president and realized that SGA's highest office was attainable, if I began to plan immediately. Students vote for candidates at Samford because of personality, campaigning, and networking, so there isn't just one way to win. I devised a four-step plan, which if followed, can elect anyone, anywhere.

The first step. Try to gain respect from at least one large political entity within your Student Government. Since we don't have political parties or run as tickets at Samford, it's important to establish yourself as an individual. I accomplished this through membership in the Senate, which consists of 46 influential campus leaders. Upon winning a seat, I immediately began voicing my opinion often in meetings and later won the "Most Outstanding Senator Award."

I also attended statewide lobbying meetings of the Alabama Student Association and met many other SG presidents and officers. After I announced my candidacy, I got a letter of encouragement from the Auburn University SG president, which made me think I could get others to support me. I solicited another endorsement from the University of Alabama student body president to show Samford students I was respected by leaders statewide at prestigious institutions. And that's what happened: several students told me these endorsements stuck out in their minds.

The second step. You have to gain "face" on campus by making your name recognizable. This is probably the most difficult of all steps.

My first two years at Samford I was a cut-up, and still am to a certain extent. Everybody knew me and felt like they could trust me, but I don't think most students really took me seriously until I was elected junior class president. That's when I toned down my antics.

The SGA president who preceeded me was very professional. The day he walked on campus, he made friends with every professor and administrator. He became so favorable in their eyes that they elevated him as a model, which in turn made the student body respect him.

I established friendships with classmates but didn't know a lot of administrators, so the doors that were open to my predecessor weren't open to me. I later realized that I had not earned the right to open those doors. Toward the end of my term, I finally made some headway. If I had it to do again, I would make more contacts with administrators before running for office. I should have written notes, paid them compliments, and set up appoint-

(From left) Brewer's father, Brewer, Samford Provost Netherton, Brewer's mother, and 1995-96 SGA President Eric Mothey after Brewer's inauguration.

ments to talk with them about important campus issues. This would have made me stand out as a concerned campus leader.

To gain visibility, I also wrote for our student newspaper, *The Crimson*, the most influential media outlet on our campus. Before the election, I visited the editor in chief and volunteered to write a bi-monthly political article. Luckily, he agreed.

I was a public administration major and a conservative, so writing a political column on a conservative campus was a "no brainer." My articles were well-read, thanks to the popularity of *The Crimson*, and students and professors began to associate my name and face with politics.

I enjoyed writing the pieces, but I had a twofold purpose. One, I was doing something personally satisfying, and two, I was getting my name and photo in the paper regularly. This exposure helped me realize my second goal.

The third step. This is the easiest step by a long shot. It is "JBFS," which means, "Just be friendly stupid." If you can't do this, then you should give up running for president. You have to be cordial to everyone. It is easy to do this with friends, but you have to follow what Jesus, the greatest leader of all time, said: "Love thy neighbor as thyself." Simply stated, be friendly to those who dislike you the most. Try not to give your enemies and opponents fuel to throw on any campaign fire. This sounds elementary, but so few follow this important ideal.

The fourth and final step. Put yourself in a position of responsibility, because when you run for president, you have to be able to prove you can handle the job if elected. I chose an interesting route to do this. I marched into the SGA president's office and volunteered to do anything he needed me to do. This accomplished two things. First, I gained an understanding of how the office operates. Second, those involved with SGA began to respect my work ethic and spirit. When you capture the confidence of the executive officers, they will begin to campaign for you without realizing it.

Once you have followed these four steps,

Brewer had professional signs printed, then displayed them in 12 prominent locations at Samford.

when it comes time to run for the presidency, your work should be almost done. Anything you do after the campaign starts is merely icing on the cake. However, I have a few suggestions, which helped me clinch the election.

Brewer's campaign tips. The first thing I did was determine if my candidacy was something others wanted. This is a risky move if you have a fragile ego, but if no one cares except you, then you should quit while you're ahead. I contacted 40 friends and acquaintances and asked them if they would help me run by attending a committee meeting. Forty-three people attended, so I knew my endeavor was more than a selfish pursuit.

Once the campaign officially started, I turned the reins over to those 43 friends. As Teddy Roosevelt said, "The best executive is the one who has sense enough to pick good men to do what he wants done, and self-restraint enough to keep from meddling with them while they do it." This is a good rule to follow once elected as well.

Sweating out the campaign. We have a four-week campaign period. The first week is used to see who's going to run, the second week is when candidates qualify, the third week is campaigning, and the fourth week is voting. Elections are held on Tuesday with runoffs, if necessary, on Thursday.

My opponent was the assistant to the SGA president. At first I thought I was going to lose, since she's very popular and was buddy-buddy with top SGA leaders. Even though she was Greek, she also was friends with many independents and was involved in a lot of non-Greek activities.

Publicity. My signs were very distinctive. Students kept coming up to me saying, "Everybody remembers your signs." I went to a local professional sign company and struck a deal. I offered to mention his business to other SGAs across the state if the owner would not only lower his rates for me, but for any student running for office. I got professional quality 4-feet by 3-feet signs as a result. Later on, a candidate for political office in a nearby city asked me where I got my signs.

My opponent also did banners and signs all over campus, but they weren't as professional. I could only afford 12 signs, so we figured out the 12 most visible places to put them. In my opponent's case, you saw her signs so many times, they became an after-thought. Mine were not sparse, but were strategically placed, so I think they got more attention.

We're only allowed to put flyers in certain places on campus. Only two are allowed per building and only in certain spots.

We didn't do newspaper ads, because they were too expensive. Three days before the elections, we put handbills in every on-campus resident's mailbox, since 82 percent of students at Samford live on campus. My opponent waited until the day before the election, so many students never saw her flyers.

I wanted to target off-campus students, so the day of the election, we had hand-outs printed to look like parking tickets and put them on every off-campus car. Each one read, "Surprise, this isn't real, but it won't hurt to vote for a fellow off-campus student." I had a few people who told me they were worried about getting a real ticket. We were supposed to get permission to use a strategy like that, but neither my opponent nor I knew about that rule at the time.

With a campaign spending limit of $250, I spent about $249.99, which I raised from my own pocket along with a few small donations from friends.

Stumping for votes. The night before the election, 40 volunteers each called at least 10 students to remind them to vote. To be tactful, my staffers didn't say "Vote for Hunter," but instead just reminded students to vote and identified themselves as Hunter volunteers. We tried to target students whom I didn't know personally.

I also spoke at nearly every fraternity and sorority chapter meeting. Of the seven sororities, I spoke to six — my opponent was a sister in the seventh, and I chose not to speak to that one. I also spoke at all six fraternities. Fortunately, I knew the presidents of all of them, so I called to ask for permission.

My volunteers and I also sent letters to every non-Greek campus organization and spoke to about nine or 10, including the Baptist Student Union Choir which has around 100 members, mostly independent politically. The director said I was the first and only candidate ever to speak to that group since she had been there.

Debates and media coverage. At Samford, all students have to attend either or both Monday or Wednesday convocations. You have to attend 64 over your college career to graduate. Typically, we have five-minute speeches during one Wednesday "convo" at

Reed Chapel, which holds about 700 students.

My theme was making SGA "your" SGA. The president before me was friendly with the University president and was popular because he was an intelligent SGA president. The administration used him as a role model for the university, so a lot of students felt he was almost like an employee of the school, rather than a student representative. I emphasized the fact that "A vote for me is a vote for you."

Without warning during the speeches, my opponent was derogatory against me and slung a little mud, saying I didn't have enough experience. I still don't know why she did this, but I suspect she saw that she was going to lose and was making a last-ditch effort. The problem was that she didn't even know what I had done. As the SGA president's assistant, she wasn't even aware that I had been sending me to meetings on behalf of Samford all year. People left thinking "Whoa, I know who I'm voting for." After the elections, she stopped me one day and said that she didn't mean anything by it. It wasn't a personal attack.

There was a debate on the campus TV station SNN, the Samford News Network. We also had a separate debate forum that ran daily a week before the election. On election day, SNN ran the program back-to-back all day long. I felt like I made a good impression — my goal had been to avoid making a fool of myself. I hoped this show would be an outlet for students to get to know me a little bit.

Summary. The office of SGA president is one of respect and responsibility at our school. It's something you shouldn't enter into blindly. I feel that my four steps will guide you down a path to success. Remember, the fact that you're reading this book means you're already well on your way, because success is "planted in the field of preparation."

Contact: Hunter Brewer
Address: 195 Piney Knoll Dr., Gadsden, AL 35901
Phone: (205) 442-7452
E-mail: hbrewer@wwisp.com

A Last-Minute Candidate Wins At La Sierra University

By Shasta Emery
1995-97 Student Association President
La Sierra University, California

Introduction

Emery, 20, served two years as Student Association president. While she doesn't plan to run for a third term, Emery will stay active on campus as a volunteer at the Riverside Rape Crisis Center, a forward on the varsity basketball team, and as the youngest board member of the local Chamber of Commerce.

After graduating in June 1998 with a degree in communications, Emery dreams of creating an outward bound camp for at-risk youth.

How Emery Became the First Female Freshman President

"You should run for president, we can't let only the guys run," I said half-heartedly to an upperclasswoman sitting next to me in chemistry class, only days before the upcoming spring elections in February 1995.

She laughed and challenged me, "Why don't you run then?"

The thought hadn't even crossed my mind before, but it got me thinking. Over the next 24 hours, it wouldn't go away even though I reminded myself that I was only a second-quarter freshman. Until then, I had attended only one Student Senate meeting. I told myself that others had more experience and knew the ropes better. I also noted that I would be leaving immediately after the elections to spend the spring quarter in Paris, so I wouldn't even be there to shadow the current president. Despite all of this, what made me finally decide to go for it was a couple of senior guys telling me I didn't stand a chance because I was so young.

With elections only two days away, I strolled into the Student Life office and requested an application to run. The whole time I was thinking that I should come to my senses and realize that I have no business running for president as a first-year student. The secretary looked at me carefully to make sure that I wasn't joking, then cautiously handed the form to me.

We do have competitive elections here at La Sierra, a school with 1,600 students, 35 campus clubs, and about 20 SA positions. At election time, posters, lawn signs, and flyers cover the campus, friends campaign for their favorite candidate, and guesses are made about who the winning team might be. Everybody else campaigned, but my name wasn't cleared as a candidate until the day before the election, so I didn't do much of anything. La Sierra, by the way, has no limits on campaign spending, but most students only spend money on making copies. There's also no set campaign period — you can start campaigning as far in advance as you want. Most candidates wait until a few weeks before the election to start their push, as they don't want to appear too eager and aggressive.

Since I waited so long to decide, I had to do something to impress the student body. My only chance was to "sell myself" at the mandatory weekly assembly. SA gets one of these each semester to conduct elections. I smiled calmly, as all of the candidates for office sat facing the student body, but inside, I thought I was going to throw up. I prayed that I would concentrate on speaking slowly since I tend to talk faster than any human ear can comprehend, especially when I'm nervous.

Originally, there were three candidates running for president, but one dropped out at the last minute, so it ended up being me against a junior honors student. At the assembly, this opponent looked nice in a suit and tie, and I sat watching him reread his notecards for the 10th time. I decided to dress casually just like I always do, hoping that students would see me as a genuine person. I was going for an image of being candid and real: "This is who I

Emery and her roommates (from left) Charisa Bauer, Emery, Allyson Hilliard, and Wendy Burns celebrate her first victory in the 1995 Student Association elections.

am, and this is who I'll be even after the election."

Turn negatives into positives. Since people had told me that I couldn't win because I was a freshman with no experience, I knew what I had to prove in my speech. If a few people had doubts, I assumed that there would be others with similar feelings. So I planned to actually use my age to my advantage.

I closed my eyes to concentrate on what I would be saying in only moments. When it came time for my turn, I took a deep breath, closed my eyes, and prayed for peace. I stood up, and faking confidence, grabbed the microphone off the stand and greeted everyone with energy. Without notes of any kind, I started a three-minute speech. My first desire was to inform the student body that while I hadn't been involved in big leadership roles in college, I had the experience from high school and other areas of my life. By not using notes, I appeared more casual, as though I were thinking up my resume experience on the spot, in contrast to someone who needs to read off their achievements as though they can't remember what they've done. I kept that part pretty short, not wanting to look as though I were bragging.

Then I smiled and said, "The best thing is that I am a

freshman." I wish I could have seen the look on the faces of the guys who told me that I would lose because of that! I backed up my statement with reasons as to why it would be advantageous to elect a freshman rather than the traditional senior. By being a freshman, I had three things to offer. The first was that Student Associations seem to change year to year, with very little growth or continuity. By the time the president usually gets the hang of the position, it seems that the year is practically over. So by electing me into office, the student body was assured that I would at least still be on campus the year after my term to help the new person and to provide more permanence.

My second point stressed serving as a sophomore would be better than being president as a senior. As a sophomore, my schedule would still be very flexible and I could take a lighter class load if I needed to devote more time to the Student Association. A senior, on the other hand, would be busy trying to complete required classes.

My third argument was that a new student wouldn't be bogged down with the "this is what they've always done" symptom. I had fresh ideas and was ready to implement new events and energy. This feigned confidence helped warm students to an energetic and optimistic candidate with guts.

Don't make promises you can't keep. I love politics, with the exception of the fake persona which many feel they must wear to be successful. This can include making promises without the knowledge that they can be accomplished. I detest promises that are harder to keep than most candidates can imagine.

While I'm not convinced that my "platform" won the election, I did compile a list of campus complaints, such as doing away with required assembly and improving cafeteria food. I also wanted to cater more to commuter students when planning and promoting events and wanted sports to be of greater importance.

I went through the list and crossed off the items that realistically couldn't be changed. Then I chose the two or three that I would focus on while in office. If I'm going to stand up and speak for my goals, then I need to set goals that are attainable. As I said,

I didn't want to make promises, since I didn't even know exactly what the job entailed at the time!

Run on who you are. I don't think my success was because I championed these issues, but because of who I am. In the 1996 national presidential elections, it was often heard that America seemed to care less about morals and ethics in their choice in candidates. However, all I wanted was to be voted in for who I am. I'm not just talking about lifestyle and upright morals because most students didn't know me and wouldn't know if I was telling the truth or not. But I like to think that my success was based on who I showed I was through my actions. For example, if voters saw my willingness to act in risky situations, then they might believe that I would also take risks and not fear standing up for what I believe in. If I presented myself energetically and optimistically, they might think that I'm capable of presenting a positive image of our school when I travelled or worked within the community. I wanted the audience to see my strengths — it's ALWAYS better to show than tell.

Back at the speech, my opponent left his notecards on his chair when he went to the podium. I have to wonder if he did that because I didn't use any. He stumbled a bit because I dare say I took away some of his arguments by highlighting the advantage of my young age that he hoped to use against me. My advice? Try to use anything that could be seen as a disadvantage to your benefit. Everything has a bright side.

I still remember answering the phone at 11 p.m. that Thursday night back in 1995. I remember the sound of the senator-at-large's voice congratulating me on my victory. He asked me if I would be interested in the point spread; he thought it might make me happier, but I declined. I still have no idea how much I won by; it's irrelevant to me.

My first year as president taught me so much. I learned more tricks and protocols than I could ever write in a book. The knowledge of student government is far beyond anything a textbook could teach. When I attended a business class about how to manage people "out in the real world someday," I chuckled

After taking office in 1995, Emery (third from right) with members of her first SALSU team.

knowing that so much of it already applied to me. I learned to be more effective in time-management skills and at taking care of myself, as far as maintaining my grades, getting enough rest, and having time off to rest and relax.

The following year, I ran unopposed, becoming the first person to hold office for two consecutive years in the 75-year history of my school. My purpose in running the second time was to make internal changes, including redirecting some of the money in our budget to bring in more speakers. I also wanted to start a "club rush" to encourage more students to get involved, including commuters. I had dreamed of setting up a drug prevention conference, which became a reality during my second term. In fact, it was so well-attended, the administration plans to make it a mandatory annual event.

I ran for a second term because I believed a new president doesn't have the knowledge or experience to make major changes or improvements, and by the time he or she gathers those two qualities, the year is practically over. Providing the Student Association with some permanence allowed the creation of larger projects.

As I complete my second year in office in June 1997, I redefined the role of my position to be more a part of the community, rather than just the school. By no means is next year's president expected to be a board member for the Chamber of Commerce, a volunteer at the Riverside Rape Crisis Center, or a committee member on various city meetings, etc. Maybe his or her passion will extend to other equally important realms of life.

A president's job isn't just to do defined duties. A president's role as a leader is to redefine constantly his or her position to make it the best for constituents. Don't feel the need to be the angry parliamentarian with the administration. Don't think you have to shake hands and kiss babies like other leaders. When you campaign, be yourself and show them who you are. Then, you'll have no promises to live up to other than staying true to yourself.

Whether you win or lose the election, I dare say you won't regret your decision, for a true leader doesn't give up or refuse to learn from the obstacles in life.

Contact: Shasta Emery
Address: 1371 E. Bates Ave., Englewood, CO 80110
Phone: (303) 762-8770
Fax: (909) 785-2555 (at school)
E-mail: shasemer@lasierra.edu

The President Who Jump-Started Student Council at Polytechnic

By Phil Shpilberg
1995-97 Student Council President
Polytechnic University, New York

Introduction

As the only three-time student body president in Polytechnic history, Shpilberg, 22, served as interim president in 1995, then won two elections as Student Council president. He also was a peer counselor, served as chairperson of the Senior Gift Committee, and was president of the Jewish Student Union.

After graduating in June of 1997 with a bachelor's degree in mechanical engineering, Shpilberg plans a career in engineering management.

How Phil Got Student Council Going Again

I knew I wanted to be Student Government president the day I walked in the front door at Polytechnic. But to my dismay, I discovered that student government was defunct and had not operated for three years.

At first I was disappointed, but then thought of this as a unique opportunity to do something original and challenging: start a brand new student government!

Polytechnic University is a small technical school with three campuses in New York state. Each campus is somewhat independent. The Long Island campus has it's own government, while Westchester is purely a graduate and research center. I attend the Brooklyn campus which is the largest with an undergraduate student body of just over 1,000 students. More than 95 percent of these students are commuters, which is a difficult situation since most of the students don't spend their free time around school.

I knew as a freshman that I wanted to be student body president. Although we didn't have a government, I knew that the opportunity to form one would come soon enough, so I tried to prepare myself to be a strong candidate. I knew I needed to gain the respect of my peers to have a chance as a candidate for president later, so I started in a small organization. Typically, the road to the top of a smaller group is quick, and sure enough, I was elected vice president of the Jewish Student Union my freshman year, then became president as a sophomore.

Another great way to gain credibility and respect is to teach a "college assimilation" class. In my sophomore year, I became a peer counselor— one of the students who organize orientation activities for incoming freshman and transfer students. As part of this role, I taught a one-hour course, "Freshman Seminar." I also took a job as a laboratory technician in the freshman engineering department and taught a three-hour lab and a one-hour recitation each week.

Spending a total of five hours in front of freshmen weekly allowed them to know me well. Not only did getting involved help me gain visibility and respect, I also developed my public-speaking skills and got accustomed to appearing in front of large groups. It was a great way for me to make the administration of Polytechnic take notice as well.

At the end of my sophomore year, I found myself ready to take charge and make my move. I had a great relationship with the director of student activities from having worked with him as JSU president and a peer counselor. Several times, we talked about restarting student government. At the end of my sophomore year, he finally agreed, and we decided to make an attempt.

Knowing that the average student at Polytechnic wasn't very active on campus, we understood that this task was going to be challenging. We asked each student organization to send one representative to the initial meeting. We got a great response as most of the active groups participated.

In concert with Polytechnic's very best campus leaders, we

sat down and drafted a constitution, which included the purpose of the new "Student Council." It also outlined the rules for membership, leadership, and all other aspects of the group.

We realized that other schools have problems because a few major groups such as Greek organizations seem to take control of student government. It became clear that we had to do something a little different. Out of this came the idea of the Club Council— each club would send one representative to the Council. And each class level (based on the number of credits completed) would elect one representative, with the exception of the Freshman class, which would get two reps. The club and class reps would then elect the Student Council officers.

This meant that the Student Council president would be elected by about 35 students rather than by the student body at large. Each club held one vote regardless of the its number of members. The Freshman class held two votes while the Sophomore, Junior, and Senior classes each held one vote.

Once each club appointed a representative, we decided that an acting president would have to be elected until the time the government was fully formed. This interim president would be given three months to form the Council, hold class representative elections, get the constitution ratified, and establish the credibility of the Student Council with both students and the administration.

Here I saw my chance and immediately went to work. In my bid to become interim president, I needed to show several things. Most importantly, I wanted to prove that I understood the tasks described above. I tried to establish, both with the students and administration, that I was a veteran leader. I pointed to my past experience as JSU president, peer counselor, and a laboratory technician. Next, I had to show that I had goals beyond the interim position, something which my two opponents completely forgot.

I made sure I spoke to as many student organizations as possible. Polytechnic allocates three "club hours" a week. All organizations have their meetings during these hours. In the span of two weeks, I spoke to 27 out of 35 active organizations. I used five minutes in each meeting allowed. I knew many leaders from

Immediately after his first election, Shpilberg was introduced as Student Council president to Polytechnic administrators and donors at the University Club in Manhattan, New York.

past experience, so "scheduling" myself was rather simple.

On election day, each of the three candidates made a short speech in front of the acting Student Council. My two opponents spoke about how they planned to establish the Council, in general terms, citing their credentials. Their speeches bordered on the idea that because they were popular they could lead the Student Council. Both seemed somewhat unprepared because they constantly fumbled with what they wanted to say next.

On the other hand, I came with a very well-prepared speech—about a specific plan for getting started. I was clear about my objectives and exactly how I would go about achieving them. I presented my credentials and how these skills would make me effective—stating things like "My past leadership positions establish my ability to lead an organization and work with budgets and the administration. I have also learned much about long-term planning from these positions." Making these connections is something my opponents failed to do. I also presented my plan after the interim period for the Council.

The result was a narrow victory margin— I won against two opponents by the count of 13 votes to 12 votes to 11 votes— the closest possible victory. When I saw the results, I breathed a huge sigh of relief, but wasn't happy with this close win. While most students would have been thrilled, I knew that if I didn't get things done as I had promised, I'd never stand a chance in three months in the real election.

From this point forward, I was under a microscope. I knew that my opponents were waiting for me to make a mistake and would take advantage of it. To counteract this, I recruited the best campus leaders I could find to handle each specific task. I put one of these leaders in charge of setting up class rep elections.

Then I took a huge gamble when it came to the ratification of the constitution— I put one of my main opponents in charge. Many thought I was nuts— After all, she was in the perfect position to make me look bad by not finishing her assigned task.

But there was reason behind my madness: I knew that she took too much pride in everything she did to intentionally do something wrong. Furthermore, she would make herself look bad if she failed. The benefit of this move was clear to me: I looked very good by selecting one of my opponents for a key job. I also proved that competitors could work cooperatively, side by side. Many other leaders respected this move because she clearly was competent, and I was as fair and honorable because I gave her the job in the first place.

Having delegated two key jobs and keeping a close eye on progress, I worked on the image of Student Council. I sought to gain credibility for the Council and to eventually link the name "Student Council" to my own as its president. I spent most of my time making posters and writing articles for each issue of *The Reporter*, the student newspaper, to glorify this "crusade for a student voice" and to explain our progress. *The Reporter* was the greatest tool for reaching my fellow students.

I also spoke at countless faculty, alumni, and student meetings. Everyone at Polytechnic knew what was happening and most of the school was behind me.

As a result of this strategy, I scored a landslide victory, earning 83 percent of the vote in the next election (a 29 to 6 victory). Later, I was re-elected for a final term in my senior year. Winning the election in my senior year was perhaps the most satisfying of the three because I knew that I would graduate as a winner.

In my time as president, I have done many things of which I'm proud. I started the Student Council and made it powerful. Since then we have really made a difference— Student Council now controls the allocation of student activities fees to all the student groups. We got the school painted and worked toward the opening of a new student center. We took responsibility for the student awards banquet and have implemented course evaluations. We raised money through the senior gift committee, which I chaired, and reinstated the yearbook. These are just a few of the victories that occurred during my two years in office.

Being president is difficult, tedious, stressful, and at times gut-wrenching. But it's also a blast! There's nothing like seeing your name in "lights," and it's worth every difficult step. When I graduate in June of 1997, it will be a special feeling to know that I was in the driver's seat in my college career and didn't just come along for the ride.

Looking back at how I won my campaigns, I firmly believe that a good plan can win an election, because most students are intelligent enough to see through the phony candidates who just want to become president to build their resume. In addition, there is a great feeling of accomplishment when you serve your school and your fellow students. My biggest reward was when a fellow student came up to me and said "I really see a difference at Polytechnic since the Council started. I feel I have a voice now. Thank you."

Contact: Phil Shpilberg
Address: 4560 Bedford Ave, Brooklyn, NY 11235
Phone: (718) 648-6752
E-mail: phil@acm.poly.edu
Home page: http://www.poly.edu

A Five-Point Strategy for Winning at Oral Roberts University

By Matt Rearden
1996-97 Student Association President
Oral Roberts University

Introduction

Matt Rearden, 21, is Student Association president at Oral Roberts University in Tulsa, Oklahoma. In addition to his many S.A. responsibilities, Rearden works with the athletics marketing department and is actively involved in his church, Church on the Move.

After graduating in May 1997 with a degree in finance and government, Rearden plans to attend law school.

Rearden's Five Keys to Running a Campuswide Campaign

Being elected student body president at any college or university is no small task. If you're even casually considering running for office, there are several things that you should examine before entering the race. I'll give you my five-point plan, but first I want to explain how I decided to run in the first place.

ORU is a campus of about 4,000 students, with the majority living in the dorms. With so many campus residents, our Student Association plays a major role in the lives of students, so the top positions are sought after and our elections are competitive. When I decided to run for S.A. president, my position as incumbent executive vice president helped me tremendously because I was already visible to most students and had the experience of running a successful campaign the year before.

Before I decided to run, I looked closely at the office and its responsibilities. You should understand how much time you'll need to devote, because you don't want seek a position that requires your attention 40 hours a week if you can't commit to that sort of work load. I have dedicated one year of my life to serving the students, and my position literally is a 24 hour-a-day job. At ORU, every aspect of your life changes when you're elected. You're no longer John Smith the student, rather you're Student Body President John Smith.

"The greater the risk, the greater the reward," is a statement that's especially true in campus politics. Make your decision carefully and examine every aspect of the office you intend run for before you throw your hat into the race. If you determine that student leadership is right for you, it will be an enjoyable experience. But be careful — if you're not right for the job it will make you miserable.

Here are five keys that helped me win at ORU:

Key #1: People. Never underestimate the power of students who are willing to commit to a candidate they believe in. Without support, you're sunk before you leave the dock.

Immediately after deciding to run, I selected my core election staff. Five students became my close advisors months before the campaign started. They were students who would stand up to me, give good, level-headed advice, and tell me the facts straight—not just spout what I wanted to hear. These advisors also would watch the other candidate and analyze what he was doing while I concentrated on what I was doing.

These advisors were with me constantly, and together we developed a strategy for the entire campaign. It's important to make sure these few core people are diverse in both background and beliefs, and that they know the heartbeat of your campus. They don't necessarily have to be prominent "campus leaders," but they should have a significant sphere of influence.

We also recruited students whom we knew would be an asset to the campaign. Because of the residential nature of Oral Roberts University, we specifically chose one or two key people per floor to represent me during the election week. I kept them informed through campus mail and the voice mail system. They reported to a dorm chairperson who was always in close contact with me. Even though these floor representatives may seem insignificant, I have discovered that when there's a constant reminder of a candidate, especially by a peer, the effect is immeasurable. We adopted the nickname "Team Matt." By the time the campaign kicked off, I had 150 team members, which also translates into an assured 150 votes.

Key #2: Preparation. There's no substitute for proper planning. You should have a strategy ready to implement months before the campaign. To use a famous quote, "Those who fail to plan, plan to fail."

Our core of advisors and I developed a comprehensive campaign strategy, which included vision, goals, and how to accomplish each one.

I then focused my attention on executing all these well-thought-out plans. Our first priority was developing our propaganda materials. We developed a slogan, logo, and theme for the campaign, which was similar to the logo I had used in the previous campaign. I feel that the use of a logo was crucial, because no matter what people saw— a flyer, a sticker, or a poster — everything included the universal "Matt Rearden for President" logo. Even if they didn't read every flyer or brochure, over time we reasoned that voters would recognize that Matt Rearden was running for president.

With the logo completed, we designed posters, stickers, and flyers in our campaign color scheme - red, white, and blue. No matter what colors you use, it's important to use a consistent color scheme.

A slogan helps to define a candidate and what you plan to do. It should be simple and catchy but short and distinct enough to remember. The slogan I used was "The Future is NOW!"

With the logo and slogan established, my staff and I then began to put them to use on campaign materials consisting of stickers, position sheets, flyers, and posters. When we designed the stickers, it was important that they could be recognized from a long distance away. I personally used two and one-half inch round stickers with red printing and the "Matt Rearden for President" logo. These stickers were worn by my volunteers and other students to show their support. We originally printed 1,000, but as the campaign wound down, we had to print 200 more.

Next, the important position sheets took center stage. They included a picture of me, the logo, as well as detailed qualifications and ideas for the future. They were printed on 8.5" x 11" gray paper in red and blue ink. These sheets were posted on every floor on campus. It was important to put these sheets where students would read them, like bathrooms and next to elevators. The election rules at ORU only allow two posters per floor, so placement in high traffic areas was crucial.

Flyers also were important in our campaign. My goal before the campaign started was to get at least one flyer in the hand of every student, so we produced about 4,500 flyers. We produced four different flyers that were circulated. Three of them were one-third of a page and the fourth was one-quarter of a page. One flyer was a rearranged position sheet, one had campus problems and my solutions listed, another had personal testimonies about me, and the last one was a list of programs played by the campus radio station (a public service flyer with our logo printed on it).

The last campaign materials we developed were posters. They measured about 3' x 6', which was a good size to fit in many different places. In making these posters, we blew up the design on a blueprint copier and then made a poster-board stencil from that copy. When the stencil was completed my staff and I spray painted the posters in a friend's garage. We produced a total of 25 posters, which included seven extras in case some were damaged by the weather or just wear and tear and needed to be replaced.

While these materials are necessary, don't spend too much time working on them personally, because that will take you away from meeting and speaking with your potential voters.

Another tool that we used on this campaign was an internet home page. I had a talented team member who designed and maintained the site. To publicize the page, we put the address on all of my campaign materials. Surprisingly, we had a tremendous response, at least 500 hits. When you can utilize something that you opponent doesn't have, it sets you apart.

During election week, I also paid for an advertising spot on the campus radio station, which plays alternative music. A majority of students listen to it, but it hits a different crowd that we were able to reach with posters. The station manager gave me a great rate and ran our commercials once an hour. This was a fantastic way to infiltrate the dorms with my message. While we were campaigning near one of the polling places, we turned on the radio station and passersby could hear our commercials. Our opponent was caught off guard by our commercials and didn't have time to produce his own spot.

Financing your campaign is always a concern. At ORU the campaign finance rules are very strict: a candidate can't spend or receive more than $300 on the total campaign. This means that even if you get all your materials donated, the total fair market value can't exceed $300. You must produce receipts for everything, from spray paint to tape for poster hanging. It's important to shop around for the best prices on printing and supplies, but it's also helpful to find an accounting major to help you prorate some of the materials you don't use. Running a campaign on a small budget brings that creativity out in many people. I was fortunate enough to have the $300 for my campaign, but you can solicit financial support from friends or organizations on campus and/or get donations from local businesses. It may not sound like a lot, but you'll be surprised how far $300 will go.

Key #3: Visibility. Let students see you, ask you questions, and get to know you. There's no substitute for talking and listening to voters. Voters have a choice. If they know you or have had a conversation with you, then they're more likely to cast their vote in your favor.

I visited the dorm rooms of every male student on campus, and I had several female team members visit every woman's room on campus. Many times I would just sit down and talk to the guys about sports or something not related to the campaign. More times than not, they would tell me "Matt, I'm going to vote for you because you're a real person who cares enough about my concerns to come to my door and ask me."

I must admit that this is one of my favorite parts of running a campaign, because I met many neat people and simply had a good time. I can't stress enough the importance of talking and listening to students— it's crucial to your success in a campaign and later on in life.

One tradition during the annual campaign week at ORU is the famous "poster sprint" — no posters can be put up before 7 a.m. on the first day of the campaign. Knowing this, I and several team members arose about 5 a.m. to stake out the prime locations, and we were able to secure most of the top spots.

It's also important to have your staff know exactly where you will be at all times. Have a schedule prepared before the week begins, but make sure you're flexible. Remember that important events always unexpectedly come up and you should be there. It also allows your staff to know where you are so that they can reach you in an emergency.

Key #4: Word of Mouth. Get your volunteers to tell their friends and acquaintances why you're the best candidate. This will sell you better than any flyer, poster, or sticker.

News spreads quickly at a smaller campus like ORU, particularly with so many on-campus students. Because our paper, *The Oracle*, is published only once a week on Mondays, it can't cover the campaign or the debate until after the elections. Unlike at some schools, our debates are fairly well attended, with 350 students, candidates, and supporters.

Debates can be important because some borderline voters will make up their minds after hearing you in person. I know for a fact that several of my opponents' volunteers switched sides after our debate.

If you're involved in any type of a debate during your election campaign period, the best advice I can give you is the advice I used. Keep it short, sweet, and to the point. Students hear lectures every day, and if you lecture them and drag your speech or answers out, they'll turn you off. Hit the issues that concern your campus, but don't bore the listeners or you will lose their votes.

Key #5: Focus. Once you decide to run for president, it's important not to let the talk of other challengers sway your conviction to seek office. I decided to run because I strongly felt that I had something to offer the ORU student body and I believed that I was the best candidate. It's not difficult to find out what others are doing, but when I heard of potential challengers, I made up my mind to stay focused on my campaign and not worry about what they were doing or planning to do. When candidates lose elections at ORU, it's usually because they concentrated too much on their opponents rather than themselves. Focus on key campus issues. This focus should carry you through your whole campaign. Let the other candidates worry about you if they want to, but don't concentrate on them.

Next, be positive and focus on yourself. Don't get in the habit of "dirty" politics, because college students have all seen that in the national political scene. Believe me, they respond better to what you can do for them than why your opponent is no good. My opponent was a good friend, and I decided early on that I wouldn't say anything negative about him during the whole campaign. If you run against someone who "slings mud," people will see through it. If you retaliate, you'll look like the attacker and turn potential voters off to your entire vision. Tell people your message, convictions, and why you're right for the position— no more, no less. They'll respect you for it and you may get their vote.

You want to focus exclusively on your campaign and its issues. I heard a speech once that defined true leadership as "not just showing or selling your objective to people, but following that objective with such fervency and passion that others jump behind you and help you accomplish it." You must believe in your campaign platform so passionately that your student body follows behind your plan. Personally, I relied on the strength of God to carry me through the campaign week. There's absolutely no excuse for lack of enthusiasm or mediocrity in campus politics. You must go for it all and run the race to win.

Relax after the voting is over. After the grueling campaign week, I won with 67 percent of the votes, with a voter turnout of 2,700 or nearly 68 percent. Voting ended at 7 p.m, then the votes were tallied in the S.A. office until about 11:15 p.m. I hung out with some friends and my brother and played pool and video games while waiting for the results. While the votes are tabulated, one "vote watcher" from each campaign is allowed to be present, and after the results were final, our watcher came out of the office, trying to keep a straight face. He walked up to me and said, "Congratulations, you're going to be our next president." Then I was swarmed with supporters and reporters and photographers from *The Oracle.*

Of course, a successful campaign can't be run by the candidate alone. I had to have qualified, committed people who were willing to give up class time, study time, and sleep to help me. It's not a one-person show, but rather a campaign for something in which many people believed. Committed students also are key to your success once you're elected. Without fellow students who believed in me and supported me during those critical months, I would have never been elected student body president.

While there's no sure formula for winning a campuswide election, the experiences that I've gained throughout my two campaigns should give you some ideas.

Contact: Matt Rearden
Address: 7 Winding Creek Way,
Ormond Beach, FL 32174
Phone: (904) 677-6859

126

The Largest Victory Margin Ever At Vanderbilt University

By Phil Ayres
1996-97 Student Government Association President
Vanderbilt University

Introduction

In addition to his duties as SGA president, Ayres, 22, serves as an NROTC midshipman and a member of the Alpha Tau Omega fraternity.

After graduating in 1998 with a degree in Human and Organizational Development, Ayres plans to be a commissioned officer in the U.S. Navy.

How Ayres Ensured His Victory As The Favorite

My road to the SGA presidency was paved with intense preparation and effort over three years. It began with choices I made in my freshman year — I joined many organizations ranging from the Inter-Residence Hall Association (Interhall) and the Alpha Tau Omega fraternity to campus political clubs. Involvement in these groups and others helped me meet many students who would open doors for me later in SGA.

My quest for the top spot began during my junior year when I pursued one of the two senate seats for the Class of 1997. During the senate campaign, I learned a valuable lesson: while ideas are important in Vanderbilt SGA elections, name recognition is equally critical. So I made sure that my name was on as many signs as possible around campus. Once elected, I fulfilled my promise of being held accountable by my class. I did regular mailouts through campus mail to friends and supporters to inform them of what I and other SGA members were doing on their behalf. Maintaining contact proved to be a tremendous aid when I decided to run for president.

Not long after winning my senate race, I was chosen by my Senate peers to serve as speaker. This position allowed me to learn much about the university while developing a grasp on what it takes to be a progressive SGA president. Through observing the successes and shortcomings of the president at that time, I was able to note what kinds of mistakes to avoid and what issues to pursue, if I eventually decided to run for president. While he had some good ideas, he didn't communicate well with fellow SGA members or the administration. I decided that my administration should reach out to other schools to get ideas and to combine our efforts on major issues.

The speaker position also allowed me to work with administrators and to find out what issues and projects they wanted SGA to tackle. Serving on committees, meeting individually with key administrators, attending university functions, and filling in for the SGA president at meetings allowed me to gain the credibility that would be beneficial later when I lobbied the administration as SGA president.

Learn from former SGA leaders. When I decided to run, I thought about what kind of president I wanted to be, as well as what kind of vice president I wanted to have. After observing the strengths and weaknesses of past presidents, I knew that I wanted to be a combination of two contrasting styles. First, I wanted to be very practical with concrete ideas for how goals could be achieved. But I also wanted to be idealistic and have a long-term vision that would transcend my one-year term of office.

Though we don't have a "party" system, the president and vice president run as a team and have to work closely together after the election. For this reason, I thought it was vital to pick someone who would be an honest and diligent partner, as well as a vibrant campaigner. For me, the choice was easy. I had worked on a number of projects with the SGA president's executive assistant, Jenny Turner. I admired her for being a hard worker, and more importantly, valued her loyalty and friendship.

Once Jenny agreed to run with me, we decided to be a team

of transition, since SGA was in dire need of long-term planning. I think this is our SGA's biggest ongoing problem. Since students typically are here just for a few years and our administration lasts only one year, it's difficult to commit to long-term goals. But we began to think about students' needs, such as the renovation of our student center and heightened campus security measures. For years, our student center has not been a headquarters for most students and organizations, except for SGA and the student paper, *The Hustler*. Instead, the center mostly had been dedicated to displaying modern art and showing movies. We believed that lobbying for a "student" center should be a long-term priority.

Though safety isn't a tremendous problem for our school, we did want to implement education and enforcement programs to make students feel more secure and make "Vandy" a more attractive home to potential new students.

During our campaign, these issues were important. But frankly, successfully "selling" our presidential team was even more important.

Even before we knew who our opponents would be, Jenny and I believed that we would be the favorites. We both had established records of service, were well-known, and were Greek. This is important since about 40 percent of our students are Greek. This also ensured that we would have a hard-working labor force for our campaign.

Our opponents were both male members of the same Greek house. That meant we would have the support of at least two houses to their one. Our opponents were also SGA outsiders, but this could work to their advantage, as it had in past elections. We decided to stress our experience and past records. This turned out to be the best strategy for us.

The biweekly school newspaper has only endorsed one candidate since I've been at Vanderbilt — typically the paper stays impartial. Most of the time, it simply reports the platforms and issues. We did try to get an endorsement by sending campaign literature to every member of *The Hustler* staff but to no avail.

SGA rules strictly prohibit any campaigning before the two-week formal period. However, we are permitted to put together a campaign structure before this period. This begins with the selection of a dedicated staff. We selected staffers from our network of friends and volunteers. Our staff consisted of 12 students, plus my fraternity brothers and Jenny's sorority sisters.

One general campaign manager handled the technical aspects: getting volunteers to make posters and setting up appointment times for my vice-presidential candidate and me to speak at various student-organization meetings.

Try TV commericals. Our second campaign manager handled the media side — this is where our campaign tried something innovative. Vanderbilt has a closed-circuit student television station, VUTV, which students often watch for current movies and the student-produced news program. We became the first SGA campaign to use television as a publicity tactic by running commercials. We wanted students to see our commercials and talk to their friends, saying "This is new and creative." We were hoping to create a buzz on campus.

The commercials featured the consistent theme: "Vote Phil and Jenny." By using our first names in all promotional materials, we hoped to keep a personal and approachable contact with students. We hoped that this would send them to the polls on election day to vote for two friends rather than distant politicians.

These 45-second commercials were produced at no cost by our communications director, a political science and theater major whose father helped with Jimmy Carter's political ads, and were run free. The commercials featured our record of past accomplishments, as well as sound bites talking about our ideas. The Beatles' song "Revolution" played in the background to convey that we were revolutionizing the way that student government did business.

Several days later, our competitors copied us, but their spot wasn't well planned or professional. They made accusations and their spots looked sleazy.

In addition to appointing two campaign managers, we also recruited students to serve as chairs for election day, publicity, and

Ayres used a consistent theme throughout the campaign, "Vote Phil and Jenny," later adding their last names to flyers and banners across the Vanderbilt campus.

polling. The election-day chairs were responsible for setting up information booths in the dining hall and organizing supporters to pass out materials. Publicity people were responsible for making signs and getting them up around campus. Signs are only allowed to be posted on trees with a maximum of one sign per tree. We're not allowed to tape or staple to trees but are permitted to tie signs around them.

Get feedback through polls. The students in charge of polling contacted students by phone and asked if they actually planned to vote, and if they did, for whom. Our pollsters went on to ask students which issues were most important to them. We used this information to respond and to direct the campaign. For example, we learned that our safety plank wasn't a priority to most students, mainly because we just don't have a big crime problem on campus, so we downplayed it.

To get publicity, flooding the campus with signs was our major focus. Knowing that we were limited to a $250 spending cap (raised from $5 contributions from friends and supporters), we made signs by hand rather than having them professionally done. This added a more personal touch to our campaign. This also turned out to be a great decision, because it also helped us recruit more supporters. I was convinced that the more students we could persuade to do volunteer labor on behalf of our campaign, the more likely they were to activate their friends to vote and to vote themselves.

The sign, flyer, and poster design scheme was simple, yet carefully selected. We were consistent in all of our materials. We had 3' x 5' signs put on trees all over campus with no other message but "Vote PHIL and JENNY SGA President/Vice-President." We wanted to develop this down-to-earth theme immediately. We also ordered an inexpensive button machine and had key supporters wear buttons to their classes.

Later on, we made signs that included our last names too, so that we could establish full-name identification. Throughout the campaign, our signs kept the same color scheme of red and blue on a white poster board. On the other hand, our opponents' signs were confusing and unrecognizable.

We definitely did not include platform planks on our signs. While signs are effective for name recognition and a concise slogan, campaign literature is where ideas should be discussed.

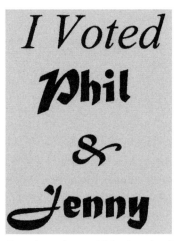

To get last-minute publicity, Ayres' staff put stickers on voters' backpacks.

We designed brochures to sell our ideas. In January, we put together a platform committee, including all sorts of campus groups, from Greek organizations to multicultural groups. They collaborated with us during a one and a half hour meeting to offer concerns and suggestions. I think this input should be a key component of any successful student government campaign — students must have a sense of ownership.

Designing our platform, choosing a staff, and assembling campaign paraphernalia was done weeks before the election, which is held on one day. This pre-planning was critical — when the day-to-day campaigning began, candidates simply don't have time to do anything except campaign. Though my school work suffered during this period, I continued to go to class. After all, SGA candidates are under scrutiny and should lead by example. If I had a lackadaisical attitude about class attendance, students and administrators might think that I lacked the ability to budget my time, and it could hurt my effectiveness later.

We also felt like making individual contact with students was critical, so we recruited point people in 50 or 60 major campus organizations to represent us. Throughout the campaign, we supplied our reps with literature that expanded on our platform and ideas. These materials were sent at no cost to us through the campus mail. Many of our materials were designed prior to the campaign cycle, but some were put together as certain issues came to the forefront during the campaign — students liked our emphasis on improving access to grades on-line, so we played that up. We also focused on the union renovation.

Just convincing students to vote was our key goal. You can campaign effectively throughout an entire election cycle, but if you ignore the students who you think will already vote for you, it could cost you the election. Jenny and I mobilized potential voters by scanning the school yearbook and identifying everyone we knew personally, then adding their names to the database, too.

Ultimately, we had 1,000 names of likely voters. Then we sent them flyers through the campus mail including the election date and voting locations. We also sent them streamlined platform literature. This strategy allowed us to hold onto our main block of supporters all the way to election day.

Originally, our goal was to break the 1,000 vote barrier. Past winning teams had typically earned between 700 and 800 votes. Our well-defined strategy allowed us to garner 970 votes (or 77.8 percent) — more than any team in Vanderbilt SGA history and also the largest margin of victory. Voter turnout was about 25 percent, about five percent higher than in recent elections. Undoubtedly, our strategy of staying in touch with potential voters reminded students to vote.

Despite all of our pre-election work, there's no doubt that who wins and who loses is decided on election day. Our team gave "I voted Phil and Jenny" campaign stickers to hundreds of students. By the end of the day, we saw these stickers on backpacks all over campus, which also was a reminder to students who hadn't yet voted.

To get the best location possible for our information booth in the dining hall, we got there at 7 a.m. when the dining hall opened. This is important, because SGA rules prohibit campaigning within 30 feet of a voting booth — so we set up 31 feet away.

At the end of a long election day, the hard work paid off with our victory. The election results were announced in front of the SGA office, where all the candidates and supporters are crowded into one hallway.

Even with all of the careful preparation in the world, you must realize that everything isn't going to go according to plan. You should be ready to adjust your strategy accordingly and be flexible. You also need to realize that you're dealing with students who are trying to balance social lives and tough academic schedules. Ultimately, you have to cater to their needs, whether you're dealing with staff or the typical voter. You should always ask: "What can I as the candidate do for each person, so that he or she can get the most out of this experience?"

Always review the needs of your constituents. And remember that your job is to lead and serve the student body. Having a thoughtful, well-planned, and informed campaign will help you win, but only a progressive agenda can make you an effective president. Getting elected shouldn't be your major goal — leaving a legacy of service to your student body should be.

Contact: Phil Ayres
Address: 4108 Marydale Dr., Nashville, TN 37207
Phone: (615) 322-2436 (student affairs office at Vanderbilt)
E-Mail Address: ayresps@ctrvax.vanderbilt.edu

A Returning Student Wins at Florida Community College at Jacksonville

By Marcus J. Pina
1996-97 Student Government President
Florida Community College at Jacksonville, Kent Campus

Introduction
Pina, 40, enrolled at Florida Community College at Jacksonville (FCCJ) after serving 20 years in the U.S. Navy. At FCCJ's Kent Campus, Pina is active in Phi Theta Kappa, is a student member of the President's Advisory Council, and serves on the College Curriculum Board.

After graduating in December 1997, he'll continue pursuing a bachelor's degree in secondary education at the University of North Florida. After teaching for a few years, he plans to earn a master's degree in deaf and disabled education.

How Pina Campaigned As A Non-Traditional Student
If you had asked me a year ago what I thought about the Student Government Association (SGA), I would have looked at you with confusion and asked, "This campus has a student government?" If you weren't one of a select few students, you knew nothing about SGA because it wasn't a very visable organization. After attending a meeting and seeing that there were many important issues concerning students, I decided to get involved.

During my first few weeks, I found that FCCJ has four campuses and each has its own SGA which operates independently. I soon realized that the Kent SGA was completely different from the other four campuses in terms of leadership and goals.

During the next two months, I decided I no longer wanted to be a member of our SGA because of the lack of leadership qualities in the current president. Despite many concrete suggestions made by her officers and other students on how to improve, her lackadaisical style meant important work was done at the last minute, which was frustrating and caused unnecessary stress for everyone. Nothing seemed to be well thought-out.

I felt that my skills weren't being utilized and decided to quit SGA. Let me say, I wasn't your average community college student; while the demographics at FCCJ show the average student is 28 years old, I'm 40.

Two fellow SGA officers asked me to stay and to seriously consider running for president. At this point, as all candidates need to do, I had to consider why I would want to be president, what I would want to accomplish, and how much time and energy I would need to perform my duties. After a month, I decided to stay on with SGA and run for president.

I knew winning this race would be no small feat. The current president, also a non-traditional student, had been involved with Phi Theta Kappa and had worked her way up from SGA secretary to president over the previous 18 months. At the time, I was just like any other student — I went to classes, did research in the library, went to study groups, and then headed home to start the same routine again the next day. What I needed was a structured campaign that would inform the students of who I was, what I stood for, and what I would do for them.

Before campaigning for any SGA position, FCCJ requires that you first submit your nomination package. You have to meet scholastic qualifications, gather 50 student signatures, and get clearance from the student activities director. We aren't allowed to campaign until a month before the election, which is held in April on a Thursday and Friday.

To get a jump on my opponent, who was seeking reelection, I needed to capitalize on her weak time-management skills and the overconfidence she seemed to display about being reelected. I still don't know why she had this attitude — she had not been elected president the year before, but had moved up when the current president left in mid-term.

In addition to making a pledge to the entire FCCJ student body, Pina tried to personally meet as many students on campus as he could during his campaign.

While there are many steps, forming a campaign committee is the most critical part of your game plan. I was fortunate to have the help of two fellow students, Tony Rodriguez and Paul Hill. We learned the rules on running for office as posted by the school and the elections committee.

Get support from the faculty. I decided that my first step shouldn't be to go directly to the student body, but to contact the faculty on campus and introduce myself. So I prepared a letter informing them of my leadership qualities, my belief in teamwork, and the importance of faculty and SGA working together. Most importantly, I emphasized the point that our campus was more than just students and faculty; it was a combination of both, including our administration, that makes a campus good or bad. I personally addressed a letter to each faculty member and signed every one.

Through this touch, I wanted to let each faculty member know this was not just another "campaign form letter." I ran off about 140 letters — one for every faculty member except for adjuncts. I personally delivered them to faculty members' offices, either giving it to him or her, or sliding it under the door. I took the letters around at about 3 p.m. after most classes were over for the day. The first thing I wanted each instructor to see in the morning was my envelope. About 80 percent found their letters that way, while the others were in their offices when I delivered the letter. This strategy paid off immediately. Three faculty members invited me to speak to their classes about my beliefs and the upcoming elections. Additionally, one student told me that her professor had made copies of my letter and had passed them out in her classes.

The next step was to inform the student body about my qualifications. While brainstorming several different methods, we decided that the best tactic was to post flyers on campus. In preparing these posters, I decided to use strong, short sentences and leave out flowery adjectives. Additionally, I included my military service as a way of showing leadership ability. Jacksonville is a large military town with two nearby naval air stations. By emphasizing my military service, I hoped to connect with active-duty military personnel, their spouses, and their children who were attending classes.

The location of these flyers on campus was another important decision. My campaign committee and I felt that posting a lot of flyers everywhere for almost three weeks would become an eyesore and students would not stop to read them. Our campus has five entry points from the parking lots and we decided to concentrate on those areas. We also posted flyers around the large courtyard where students gather to talk and walk to the different buildings.

Our last promotional idea was to post flyers in the restrooms. Starting at 6 a.m. one day, we hit every restroom, both men's and women's. In the men's restrooms, we posted them above the urinals, while in the women's restrooms we posted them just inside the stall doors and next to the mirrors. There's no formal policy at FCCJ about where we can and can't put flyers. This restroom strategy also paid off; students started to ask "Who is Marcus J. Pina?" In a couple of my classes, students commented that my restroom flyers were "good reading while I'm taking care of business, if you know what I mean."

Because our campus has lots of red-brick buildings, I used black letters on white paper, which helped our flyers stand out. My opponent used earth colors, which blended in with the background.

After we had done all the above, my opponent finally started her campaign. One advantage I had was that she had procrastinated. I had started about a week and a half ahead of her. I think she thought she had the votes of several major groups in her pocket, so she didn't feel pressured to campaign as aggressively.

Her posters reflected "I", while my posters reflected "We." This I turned to my favor when talking to students on campus. I informed them that Student Government was not an "I" association, but a "We" organization and the "We" would be placed back into Student Government if I were elected.

Don't bother students. Unlike my opponent who campaigned in the cafeteria and library, I felt that as a student, I wouldn't want to be interrupted while eating or studying. This worked against her as students later came up to me, saying they felt she was rude to disturb their meals and study time.

As election day grew closer, things did get nastier and accusations were made. My opponent accused me of having someone take down her posters, of constantly contradicting her decisions as SGA president during meetings, and of using personal information against her. While all these accusations later were proven to be false, they did get the reaction she wanted — the impression that I was running a dirty campaign. One of the other campus presidents even told me he had heard rumors that I was being negative. All of my opponent's accusations came at a time when we were one week away from debating our positions and issues before the student body, so the rumors were disconcerting.

Debate if you have the chance. But make sure you learn about past SGA projects and issues. During the day, I stopped by and talked to groups of students who were waiting for their classes to start or were just talking to each other in the courtyard. I asked them what they thought of SGA and what they wanted to see accomplished.

My next step was to make an appointment with the campus president just before the debate so I could have updated information on the topics that concerned students. I was fortunate to have an appointment with our president one hour before the debate, so I was able to find out specifics on certain issues that involved campus projects, child-care services, and the proposed parking lot expansion. These issues were a part of our debate and I was able to have before me the latest information. The debate was held between classes in the courtyard, and at any given time, there were from 75 to 100 passersby in attendance.

Also, never underestimate the importance of your delivery at the debate. Most students understand that not everyone is comfortable with talking to large crowds, but there are certain things you shouldn't do. For example, my opponent shouted into the microphone and it appeared that she was yelling at the students. I took this as a cue to lower my voice to a normal speaking manner when answering my questions. After the debate, I had one student walk up to me and state that he was going to vote for me because I wasn't yelling at him.

Our school paper, *The Campus Voice*, was anti-SGA and unfortunately didn't cover anything at any of the campuses, before or after the elections.

With two weeks to go, it was time to walk up to students and meet them. If you're given the opportunity to give a quick five-minute speech in a classroom, take it. My professors let me talk to my classes, including my intermediate algebra class. Later on election day, lots of the 28 students in my class said they voted for me.

During the week before the elections, we came out with voting badges for students to wear. Our badges simply stated, "Want the Job Done Right? Vote for Marcus Pina." Instead of just giving them to everyone, we only passed them out to 200 students who wanted to wear them.

Things were coming down to the wire and I was still worried that not enough students knew about me. During the campaign, I had tried not to make things too complicated, and came up with two ideas for election day. Our first idea concerned the fact that our campus has only one way in and one way out. We placed two large campaign posters on sticks and stuck them into the ground at the entrance. No one could drive onto campus without seeing my name.

Make a pledge to the students. The second idea included preparing a written pledge to the students, which I called "My Commitment." I said if the students elected me, I would ensure they would receive all information concerning their rights and privileges as students and legislative updates on existing laws or proposed laws that affect their education. I also informed them that if I didn't fulfill my commitment, I would return all money received for my tuition and books at the end of my term. I signed the pledge, made over 1,000 copies, and with the help of my volunteers, we stood at the different entrances of the school between 7 to 10 a.m. and gave them to students. Handing students this pledge did more for me than I could have imagined. I truly believe that this last effort put me over the top with voters.

This was supported by the fact that my victory margin over the incumbent was almost three to one. With a total voter turnout of 382 (or total turnout of 7.4 percent), I won with 294 votes (or

MY COMMITMENT

"I commit the following to the Students of Kent Campus', you will receive, if elected to the Office of Student Government President, all information surrounding:

- Legislative Updates on existing Laws and proposed Laws that affect your RIGHTS and PRIVILEGES as a STUDENT;

- Curriculum Changes affecting deletions or additions made to the school's catalog before it is published;

- PROMULGATION of all issues arising from Kent Campus' President Advisory Council that effect student's studies and welfare.

- Advance Publication on dates and times when SGA meets to assist you in planning your schedule so you may attend and voice your concerns and ideas, and

- Expeditious promulgation of all information that affects students on our campus. It is time we rid ourselves of the habit of waiting too long or waiting until the last minute before publicizing information, no matter on small, to our students.

I will fulfill the duties of President and my commitment to you. **If I do not - - I will return all grant monies received for my tuition and books based on my position as President at the end of my term.**"

MARCUS J. PINA
Candidate for
Student Government President

76 percent) while my opponent had 87 votes, with one undecided voter.

Since winning the election, SGA has been making good on its commitment to our students. On the day I officially took office, May 8, 1996, we prepared and mailed over 5,600 letters to students with updated information on legislative issues and voter registration and announced our program to raise money for a Kent Campus SGA Scholarship. Most importantly, we stressed the point that SGA belonged to them. Every letter was signed by each of the officers.

We asked the FCCJ Board of Trustees to allow students to have a say or an "ownership" of how the projected revenue from a recent tuition increase should be spent. Kent Campus student leaders hold the majority of seats on college-wide committees and we're becoming active with community businesses and charitable organizations. Because we're aware that the majority of our students work to support themselves through school, we wanted them to know about the many different opportunities they have here, such as the numerous campus events and clubs and organizations that are offered. So we adopted a slogan, "Make College More Than Just Attending Classes."

When I made the decision to run for president, I knew it would take dedication and commitment by both the officers and myself to change SGA. I wanted a productive team that would make a difference on our campus. After just one term, we have successfully moved from students saying, "What SGA?" to students knowing they have a student government working for them.

Contact: Marcus J. Pina
Address: 5327 Timuquana Road #140,
Jacksonville, FL 32210
Phone: (904) 779-1597

A Veteran Leader Wins at Barnard College

By Michelle Katz
1996-97 Student Government Association President
Barnard College, New York

Introduction

During her four years at Barnard College and at the Jewish Theological Seminary of America, Katz, 22, served as both treasurer and president of the Barnard Student Government Association, was treasurer and president of the Quad Dormitories, and was an Orientation sponsor.

In May 1997, Katz graduated with a degree in political science from Barnard and a BA in Modern Jewish Studies from JTS. She now works at Edelman Public Relations Worldwide in New York City.

How Katz Moved Up the Leadership Ladder

Ever since I entered Barnard, I was impressed with the school and wanted to contribute and make a difference. Barnard College is the all-women's school affiliated with Columbia University in New York City. With only 2,200 students, it's very easy to get involved. Everyone I know is in some club or activity. I have yet to meet a Barnard student who has extra time on her hands.

At Barnard, there also is considerable interaction among administrators, faculty, and students. For example, all search committees are "tri-partite." Almost every committee on campus, from admissions to student life to policy and government relations, is comprised of professors, students, and members of the administration. I believe that Barnard values the ideas and opinions of its students. I knew that being more involved in school would mean that I could really impact Barnard's future.

"Campaign" informally before you announce. In all three years before I ran for SGA president, I was involved in numerous organizations and earned positions with progressively more responsibility. I had held at least one titled position on campus since my first year.

In my first year, I won the position of treasurer of the Quad Hall Council. In this position, I planned programs to make dorm life more fun and meaningful for the 1,300 students in the "Quad," made up of the four biggest dorms on campus.

It was then that I started understanding that student leaders at Barnard can be more than figureheads — they can affect a lot of positive change for the student body. And I reasoned that if I could make dorm life better for Quad students, I should be able to improve the overall campus as SGA president.

Around this time, I casually started letting people know that I was interested in getting involved in SGA, maybe even running for president. The more I thought about it, the more I started talking about it — in classes, at parties, and in other social situations. In retrospect, I can see how this informal campaigning really was extremely helpful during the actual election.

Once I announced my candidacy, I found out that there was only one other presidential candidate — she also was involved in campus life and ran many important campus activities such as Springfest and Orientation. As a junior, she also served as the SGA Programming Representative.

Obey the election rules. Barnard elections are run by two current SGA members, the senior and junior representatives to the Board of Trustees, who serve for two years. These two officers determine election rules, including when and how voting will be held.

As at most schools, each candidate at Barnard is required to attend a mandatory information meeting, submit two copies of a platform of no more than 150 words, provide a photo, and sign a contract stating her intentions to run. Elections are held the week after spring break, usually at the end of March.

We were allowed to begin campaigning a week before the

Katz used quotes from famous people saying ridiculous things about women in her flyers. Only 20 flyers were allowed to be posted around the Barnard College campus.

elections, which were spread out over three days. The voting booths were in the student center during the day, in the dining hall at dinner, and in the lobby of one of the dorms in the evening. No candidate was permitted to be within 30 feet of the polls unless she actually was voting.

With respect to campaigning, each candidate was limited to 14" x 22" flyers and only 20 may be posted on campus at a time. Leaflets, cards, mass phone-mail messages, token gifts, newspaper ads, machine-made buttons, and any other form of advertised media were not permitted. In addition, all flyers have to be produced on recyclable paper. We also were not allowed to speak to classes or ask professors to endorse us. Every day the Elections Commissioners went around school and checked to make sure that everyone was following the rules. I think these restrictions were intended to level the playing field so that money does not play a role in who gets elected. The rules were so stringent, however, that some students didn't even know there was an election going on.

To increase awareness of the election as well as the candidates' visibility, the Election Commissioners sponsored two forums in which candidates had two minutes to give a speech and then fielded questions from the audience. Even though about 200 to 300 students attended both events, I don't think the forums impacted voting much. Most students weren't listening, but instead were eating lunch or talking with friends.

Prior to the elections, each candidate had to prepare a platform of 150 words, which then was incorporated into packets given to students when they went to vote. My platform stressed that I had a broad conceptualization of SGA and what changes needed to happen, such as redefining the responsibilities of the positions on the SGA board, organizing the office, and working on the internal structure of SGA. I also said that I planned to work on larger issues, such as increased student participation in campus activities, which is a goal I accomplished during my tenure as president. My opponent's platform didn't differ significantly from mine. We were both active on campus and wanted to improve SGA. We were aware of the role SGA currently had on campus, and we both envisioned an SGA that was more in touch with the student body.

Three weeks before the election, I began planning in earnest. As SGA treasurer, I knew many of the campus organization leaders and understood their frustrations with SGA, as well as their needs. Many students felt that SGA was removed from the student population and didn't completely represent students. This probably was reinforced by the fact that few students really knew what SGA did. I promised to fix or at least improve some of these problems as president by focusing on increased student participation in communicating with administrators, as well as by focusing on general public relations for SGA to let everyone know about our work.

I also contacted some of the past SGA presidents for advice. They gave me helpful hints, including recommending high-traffic areas around campus to hang my posters, which I did with the help of my brother, sister, and friends.

Choosing a campaign theme. In designing my posters, I wanted a look that would be witty and would catch attention, something that would look professional and well-thought-out. My friend and I came up with an idea to include lots of my previous quotes about campus organizations that had appeared in the campus papers, demonstrating how I had helped each of these groups as SGA treasurer. We also planned to include Supreme Court cases ruling against women on our flyers, to show that despite these decisions, women have come a long way. Unfortunately, neither of these ideas panned out. When we went through the papers I had collected throughout the year, we realized that I had been quoted about only a few groups on campus, and these groups already were supportive. As for the Supreme Court cases, I realized that counter to my perception, in reality there really weren't many cases decided against women. So instead of trying to make these ideas work, I used quotes by famous people saying ridiculous things about women. For example, one of my posters read:

"There are two kinds of women, goddesses and doormats."
—Pablo Picasso, Spanish Painter
Breaking Down Barriers
Continuing the Barnard Tradition
Michelle Katz for SGA President

I had about eight different posters and made sure to get at least 40 copies printed so that if any were taken down, I would have enough to have 20 posters hanging.

I originally thought that these posters would be eye-catching enough, but after I saw my opponent's, I realized I would have to enhance mine. My opponent had bright posters which included colorful collages made out of pieces of magazines. So I took down all of my posters one night and used highlighters to make a box around my name, added my picture, and also added an index card which said when and where to vote. That same night, I put my posters back up.

Don't lose sleep over the newspapers. *The Columbia Spectator*, the daily paper of Columbia University, endorses candidates during elections for both Columbia College and for Barnard. The two schools are different and distinct, and many Barnard students think *The Spectator* doesn't always give an accurate picture of the issues going on at Barnard. I was nervous about not getting *The Spectator* endorsement, but my concerns were eased when a past SGA president advised me that the endorsement doesn't greatly impact election results.

When I went to *The Spectator*'s office, I was under the impression that the editors would be asking me questions. Instead, the tables were turned and the 15 editors asked if I had any questions for them. I briefly felt unnerved and intimidated, but finally got to tell them about my platform and what I wanted to accomplish.

Based on this "interview," it wasn't a surprise that I didn't get *The Spectator* endorsement. Although this whole process was frustrating, ultimately the former SGA president's advice rang true — *The Spectator* endorsement didn't impact the election results.

Afterwards, I went to my interview at *The Barnard Bulletin*, our weekly newsmagazine. There, I answered questions and spoke about my platform.

Both campus papers had a spread on the candidates before the election. *The Spectator* asked us to give an answer to one question, while *The Bulletin* summarized our interview responses and printed our platforms.

The next hurdle I faced was during the second day of elections. Rules do not allow candidates to send phone-mail messages endorsing any particular candidate. Some of my friends had contacted groups in which they were active and asked members to vote for me, which was not in accordance with election rules. My resident advisor also asked me to let her know when and where the election would be held.

At 8 a.m. on the second day of elections, I was informed that my opponent was bringing me up on disciplinary charges, saying that I was leaving messages all over campus telling people to endorse me. A guilty verdict would have meant disqualification.

The Deans and the Election Commissioners questioned everyone who sent messages, and finally at 11 p.m., they dismissed the charges.

Campaign one-on-one in the dorms. The last thing I did in my campaign was knock on all of the first-year students' doors during election days. Because of my previous SGA involvement, I was very visible on campus. Still, knocking on doors and introducing yourself to strangers is nerve-wracking, because you don't know how people will respond. I spoke to some students who had blank expressions and honestly didn't care, but a few students did engage me and asked how to get involved in SGA. Having personal contact can be just as important as campaign posters and a platform.

As the campaign neared the end, I had to skip a few classes, but first I cleared this with my professors. I made up all of the work I missed after the election.

Katz's friends decorated her door in the Quad residence hall after hearing of her election victory.

The results. On the last day of elections, the voting ended at about 2 p.m. For two hours, the commissioners tabulated the votes, and finally, at 4 p.m, I got a phone call announcing that I had won. Leading up to the results, I hadn't been able to sleep, so I was relieved and exhausted at the same time. Later that night when I returned from a meeting, my friends had decorated my door, put balloons in the hallway, and bought me a bottle of champagne.

Despite all of our efforts to get students to vote, of the 2,200 students, only 12 percent actually voted. I got 148 votes and won by 25.

I knew this campaign would be tough, but I never expected the effect it would have on me. For two weeks, I couldn't sleep. I was nervous and couldn't concentrate on anything. My self-esteem and confidence level were in total flux, and I ended up crying more in those two weeks out of anxiety than I did in all three previous years that I was in school.

Running for president was one of the most trying, yet greatest learning experiences that I have ever had, in spite of all the hardships. Even if I hadn't won, the experience of running would have taught me important lessons about putting myself on the line for something I really believe in. I'm glad to say that during my tenure, we changed many election rules, which doubled voter participation this year. I hope this trend will continue, as we've laid the groundwork for a more active campus and are encouraging more students to get involved with our Student Government Association.

Contact: Michelle Katz
Address: Barnard College, Office of Alumni Affairs,
3009 Broadway, New York, NY 10027
Phone: (212) 854-2005

An Incumbent Runs Unopposed at Randolph-Macon Woman's College

By Eden C. Ezell
1996-97 Student Government President
Randolph-Macon Woman's College, Virginia

Introduction
In addition to her duties as president, Ezell, 22, served as student representative to the Board of Trustees, was a member of the Facilities Planning Committee, and served on the Institutional Planning Committee.

Since graduating in May 1997 with a degree in biology, Ezell works as a legal assistant at a law firm and plans to go to law school.

How Ezell's Leadership Experience Left Her Unopposed
During the weeks before I won office as student body president in March 1996, I was busy talking to students about the upcoming elections. However, I wasn't campaigning to get others to vote for me — in fact, no campaigning of any kind is allowed on our campus. Additionally, our enrollment is so small that nine times of out 10 your opponent is a friend. It's very difficult to say, "Vote for me and not for her." Instead, it's easier to leave it to the potential voters' good judgement.

Instead of campaigning for myself, I was encouraging other students to run for office. On a primarily residential campus with approximately 725 students, it takes a lot of work just to find candidates willing to commit to yet another activity.

In the past, many elected positions have been unopposed, but we usually have at least one woman who is interested in each of the jobs. As SG vice president at the time, I hoped that the new SG constitution had created enough excitement among students so that all 23 elected positions would be contested. I spent most of my time before the election speaking one-on-one to potential candidates, explaining why they should get involved in the "new and improved" student government.

As the deadline for declaring my candidacy approached, I realized that as a presidential candidate, I would run unopposed. While most people would have been ecstatic to hear that news, I was disappointed. I also had been unopposed the previous year in seeking the vice presidency. I believe now, as I did then, that students should have the chance to choose among candidates to find the one they think will best represent them.

Why did no one run against me? By the time Randolph-Macon students are in their senior year, they already have established themselves in specific extracurricular activities. As a rising senior, you finally can run for the SG presidency. Underclasswomen can't be SG president or serve as either of the two judiciary chairs. We also have a "mutually exclusive" policy for leadership positions, which means that students may not hold two major campus leadership positions simultaneously. This rule encourages more students to get involved on campus.

I think many students assumed I would run, and they probably felt I was capable of doing the job. Maybe the students thought a student who had been involved in SG the previous year would have a grasp of the issues and demands of the job. Additionally, many of Randolph-Macon's junior class members study abroad, which limits the pool of potential candidates. Many juniors who were off-campus that spring would have been wonderful candidates, but they had to be on campus during the mid-March elections to be eligible.

The time commitment also has a lot to do with choosing whether to run for such a tough job. When I left office in April, I wanted to sleep for a month. Many potential candidates think long and hard about the number of hours required to do the job to make sure they don't overcommit.

What made me decide to run? As a first-year student, I never imagined I would serve as SG president. I had been president of

Key Club in high school and knew I would get involved in college leadership roles, but I wasn't sure where or when. When I was a sophomore, the SG president lived next door to me. She frequently suggested that I should run for vice president, saying I would be a really good candidate.

There's no doubt I was visible on campus. I was a student representative to the family weekend committee and served as a campus tour guide. The SG president also had seen my work on a strategic planning committee and said, "We need you to do more on this campus. You need to be more involved." And I said, "Well, OK." It was almost that simple.

Before officially declaring my candidacy, I considered the positive and negative aspects of the job. I wondered if I wanted to devote 20 to 25 hours each week of my senior year to service as SG president. The more I thought about the possibility, the more I realized how much I had to offer by seeking office.

I felt the experience I had gained as vice president, in particular implementing the revised constitution, would serve me well. But what made me want to run most was my desire to give back to the

All SG candidates used buttons to promote the upcoming elections.

school that had already given me so much.

The "campaign" that's not really a campaign. Even though we don't have a formal race at Randolph-Macon, you still have to declare your candidacy and complete several forms before the final deadline to be eligible. You have to file a letter of intent, a photo, a petition signed by fellow students who attest that you're a "suitable person to hold office," a qualifications sheet, a signed contract, and a personal statement — the latter of which is the closest thing we have to "campaigning." This is your opportunity to tell voters what you're going to do for them and the College.

Each candidate's information is then printed by the Dean of

Students and the Elections Committee on an 8 1/2" x 14" poster. We don't have to spend any money — everything is handled for us by the Committee. On our pedestrian campus, the two highest traffic areas are the dining hall and the Main Hall lobby. Naturally, posters are displayed in these two places.

I began the candidate process by finding 30 fellow students to sign my petition. Many of my friends and classmates offered to sign, but I wanted to find students whom I didn't know. I hoped to encourage some of these students to run for office, and it worked. This year, three of the students I talked to last year decided to give it a shot.

I had another unique way to gather signatures, which also encouraged more students to vote and eventually run for office. A friend also was running for office, but she was ill during most of her candidate process. So I helped her get signatures as we got ones for our own petitions.

Next, I had to fill out the candidate information sheet and write my personal statement. My strategy was to keep responses as brief as possible so that passersby could stop, glance at the information, and have a good sense of my qualifications. There really weren't that many hot issues. I pushed the fact that I was trying to increase SG's effectiveness and credibility, mainly by encouraging more students to get involved.

Finally, with everything submitted, I was official. As is typical, I wasn't alone as an unopposed candidate. Of the 23 available positions, 10 were unopposed and five were unfilled. Again, the lack of competition can be blamed on rigorous academics, students' involvement in other activities, and close-knit friendships among several capable potential candidates. With such a small student body, it's inherently difficult to recruit women who are willing and able to add more activities and responsibilities to their already full calendars.

Getting more students involved. When I served as vice president, the SG constitution was in suspension as we evaluated the best way to get more students involved. That year, we operated under a temporarily revised constitution. The old one called for

(Third from left) SG Senator Kim Snow, President Eden Ezell, and Senior Class President Jenny Wiley participate in a commencement tradition, Daisy Chain, at Randolph-Macon.

about 50 representatives in both the legislative and executive branches. Based on our enrollment, these numbers just weren't realistic. With this in mind, the new version called for two smaller groups, the four-member Executive Committee and the 17-member Senate. We felt that a close model of the U.S. Constitution would be more effective and more easily understood. This proved to be true, as students approved the new constitution in March 1996. The next step was to encourage more students to become candidates.

Promoting the elections. The Elections Committee put up signs announcing the election date and locations of voting booths. During the week preceding the election, the Committee frequently sent broadcast e-mail notices to remind students to vote.

The night before elections, the executive and judicial candidates gave speeches in the student center. As usual, the speeches were poorly attended, with about 25 students there, most of whom already were involved in SG.

Our campus newspaper, *The Sundial*, doesn't endorse candidates, but it does cover the upcoming elections. The editors do a "before and after" feature. This year, the race for executive secretary had three candidates, which was unusual. *The Sundial* covered that contest because it generated more interest.

Election day arrives. Although we vote on computers at two voting stations, we had to conduct three separate elections before we could meet the required two-thirds voting quorum to make the election official. The first day's voting was a wash because of computer glitches. The second day's tally was just short of quorum. Since votes on one day don't carry over to the next, we had a third election. In the final tally, approximately 500 students, or 74 percent, voted. Since then we have changed the required number of voters to 50 percent of regularly enrolled students. Some students were frustrated about having to vote three times, but the polls were located in the two busiest locations on campus.

After the polls close and votes are tabulated, candidates are contacted individually before results are announced via e-mail. When I received my official call, I was in the SG office busily working on goals for the coming year.

The experience is worth it. While I didn't sacrifice my grades to serve as president, my GPA, which was a solid "B," might have been higher had I focused only on my studies. However, serving as president taught me just as much as my classes did.

The SG president at Randolph-Macon deals with administrators, trustees, and alumnae, so this interaction must be professional. Being president contributed to my growth in a very real way. I learned how to ask and answer questions and meet other peoples' needs. At my first Board of Trustees meeting, I told a senior administrator that I felt almost selfish being the only student to meet with all of these wonderful people and to make these connections. I feel certain that serving as president made me both a better student and a more competent professional after I graduated.

Contact: Eden Ezell
Address: 5 Raintree South,
Natchez, MS 39120

The First Chicano Student Body President At Chico State

By Oscar de la Torre
1994-95 Associated Students President
California State University-Chico

Introduction

While a student at California State University-Chico, de la Torre, 25, built a strong campuswide volunteer organization, designed programs to help at-risk youth, and interned in Washington, D.C. and New York City.

After graduating in 1995 with degrees in political science and Latin American studies, de la Torre currently is studying on a full fellowship at the LBJ School of Public Affairs at the University of Texas at Austin, working on a master's degree in public affairs.

Here's How de la Torre "Applied for the Job" and Won

My quest to become the first Chicano student body president at Chico State began while serving as chair of MeChA, a campus group, in my junior year. This leadership role gave me the necessary training and enabled me to build a network of students who would be responsible for my successful campaign a year later.

Most students are indecisive about running for positions in SG or other major campus groups because they fear losing. Anyone aspiring to run for office must understand what the position entails and must have an innate desire to serve students by representing them before the administration, the community, and the governing boards of the institution.

Some students win elections only to find out later that they can't handle the rigors of the position and their courses simultaneously. Only through strategic planning and strong support from friends can you overcome the initial fears of entering campus politics.

Once I decided to run, I thought to myself, "Who will I compete against? What issues are the most important to students? What kind of posters should I make?" And most importantly, "How could I use the Associated Students presidency to bring to the forefront higher education issues relevant to people of my background?"

I based my platform on the issues I cared most about and the perceived needs of the largest student groups. On my campus, I knew from past elections that the ethnic and Greek votes were the strongest.

Apply for the job. My campaign philosophy was that I saw the position as a job I would "apply" for, and the students would "hire" me because I had an excellent work record. It was important for my campaign literature to reflect this philosophy, so I put a condensed resume, newspaper clippings, a picture, and my platform on my brochures.

All of my propaganda featured the ying-yang symbol. I wanted people to associate it with my name — a little trick I learned in a psychology class. I have no way of knowing how effective that was, but it did have people asking questions about what it meant. This allowed me to share my personal philosophy about leadership with students and it helped them to see that I was real and not just some power-hungry politician.

Anticipate criticism. To appeal to the 89 percent of the voters the admissions office identified as non-ethnic, I had to avoid being boxed in as the 'minority' candidate. I expected the opposition to criticize me for being vocal on issues of racism, equality, and other topics that could be considered ethnocentric. Previous minority presidents were not community activists like I was. Rumor had it that the opposition was going to play the race issue against me, so to dilute this character assassination tactic, I presented a progressive platform that

At California State University-Chico, former SG President Oscar de la Torre used low-cost publicity and a unique "resume" approach to win the Associated Students election.

would benefit all students, regardless of race.

The AS president holds a prestigious position as CEO of a $15 million non-profit organization, with appointments to the California State Student Association and other committees. I wanted to enter that arena, to move my platform statewide, and to influence higher-ed policy through the board of trustees and the state legislature.

Tailor your ideas to each group. I used platform issues such as student empowerment and community partnerships as talking points, not just as words to take up space on a pamphlet. Actively discussing these points gave me flexibility when speaking to diverse groups that cared about different issues. When I talked to fraternities and discussed community partnerships, I brought up the idea of a school-wide springtime event that SG could co-sponsor with Greek groups. When I spoke to community service organizations about partnerships, I talked about Christmas toy drives for poor neighborhoods.

Even though I was the only non-Greek candidate, that didn't stop me from sharing my ideas with fraternities and sororities. Being raised in a segregated Chicano community, I felt apprehensive about speaking to "white" groups. My stereotypes were crushed when I got strong acceptance and honest comments from most Greek organizations. Ironically, the only race-based question I got was posed by a member of a Hispanic fraternity.

I can't stress enough the importance of individual commitment and sacrifice in a campaign. The candidate should work harder than anyone else and should demonstrate good leadership by being considerate about volunteers' schedules and needs.

Through the solid contacts I had with other campus leaders, I was able to interrupt meetings to give quick speeches. At our school, many groups meet on weekends, so the strategy was to schedule myself to speak to as many groups as possible. I would talk to many government and history classes — most of the professors were really into it. I learned that it's smart to write your name on the chalkboard before you give a speech, so the students will remember who you are even after you're gone.

Our SG limits candidates' campaign spending to $250 each, although people get around that by having groups place "endorsement" advertisements on their behalf. To stay within my budget, I made my campaign posters black and white. It's vital for candidates to start getting publicity as soon as they're allowed to — on large campuses, name recognition is critical. I made cardboard placards with graffiti-style letters that went up on fences near campus the week of elections. A friend of mine owned a van, so we parked it in a key location with an "Oscar for Prez" poster on it.

Strike up the band. To spice up the campaign, I called my friend who was student body president from Chico High School and had him bring drummers from the marching band for a noon-time parade across campus. Many of my friends joined them, holding picket-style posters as they marched across campus. We created a minor spectacle and had people talking about what we did. The march ended at a rally organized by another group to address student issues, but since I was friends with the organizer, he let me speak. A successful campaigner knows how to utilize every event in the periphery to his or her advantage.

Election day can make or break a campaign. Students are busy thinking about everything else besides your vision on how to make your campus better. For two days, we set up shop in front of every voting booth. I was fortunate to have people who were well-liked and dedicated to work those booths. Students notice when you're supported by good people, so you automatically gain credibility with potential voters.

Campaigning for political office gives students direct training in public speaking, networking, and grass-roots organizing. Yet holding political office is not the only way to affect change or to play an important role on campus. Then again, the excitement of winning an election is even more thrilling than graduation day!

Contact: Oscar de la Torre
Address: 12527 Barbara Avenue,
Los Angeles, CA 90066
Phone: (512) 471-4557 (until 1998)
E-mail: lpkh761@uts.cc.utexas.edu

A "Lucky" Candidate Wins At California State University, Fullerton

By Vitthara Tan
1991-92 Associated Students, Inc. President
California State University, Fullerton

Introduction

In addition to serving as ASI president at California State University, Fullerton (CSUF), Tan, 27, was an officer in the Cambodian Club, a representative in the Multicultural Council, and a student assistant at the Educational Opportunity Program (EOP) office for the five years he was in school.

After graduating in 1992 with a degree in business administration and working as a claims adjuster at Safeco Insurance Companies, Tan attended Hastings College of Law in San Francisco, where he earned a J.D. degree in 1997. He took the California bar exam in July 1997.

How Tan Defeated the Greek Machine

"Where am I?," I thought to myself. "Who are all these people staring at us, some with a sympathetic look and others with a straight face?"

To students not familiar with student government, this room, where 27 students sit behind several large tables, was the place to go to get money for all campus activities. It was, of course, the chamber where the Associated Students, Inc. (ASI) held its weekly board of directors meeting.

The spring of 1990 was the first time I stood there, too timid and nervous to say anything in our plea to get $2,000 for Asian Week. Despite the fact that the event was celebrated by more than 10 Asian races, the proposal for $2,000 was narrowly rejected. As the coordinator of the Asian Week Arts and Crafts Committee, I stood there half-lost and half-shocked as we were told that our cause was not worthy.

A political novice at the time, I just didn't understand the result. Two things, though, were obvious as the board voted on the proposal: there were only two Asian board members and both belonged to Greek organizations. While I didn't understand why they turned down the proposal, I soon learned that their loyalty to their fraternity houses was more important to them than showcasing native cultures to the campus.

Our proposal's demise and the lack of representation on the ASI board motivated me to get involved. First, I was determined to get a board of directors position so that an Asian would speak on behalf of minorities the next time a similar proposal came up. But I wasn't quite sure how to get the position. I did know two things: I wasn't popular or well-known, and I was terrified of public speaking. Although I had a lot of determination and passion, how would I overcome my apparent weaknesses?

The ASI board of directors is made up of 27 members, including three members from each school who are voted in by their respective Colleges. Unfortunately for me, I was enrolled in the largest school at CSUF: the College of Business. More students meant more votes required to get elected as an ASI board member. My task was even more formidable, because I was going against the powerful Greek system.

The Greek chapter leaders meet before every election to determine which candidates should run. After a Greek candidate is named, the system informs all its members of the selection. The "chosen" candidate then receives virtually 100 percent of the Greek vote. Because of the five to 10 percent voter turnout at CSUF, it's common for a Greek candidate to be elected without much campaigning at all. That's because even though there are only about 15 fraternities and sororities, they account for an average of 2,000 voters in each election — a formidable block.

It was impossible for me to be the Greek candidate for three reasons, most obviously that I wasn't a fraternity member. In

Daily Titan

Weekend
May 3, 1991

Tan victorious in AS runoff

By Joe McDonald
Daily Titan

Vitthara Tan

After a race marred by campaign violations and the disqualification of one of its candidates, Vitthara Tan was elected on Thursday as Associated Students president for the 1991-92 academic year.

His running mate, Yusuf Motala, an AS councilmember, will be the AS executive vice president. Both terms of office begin in July.

Tan received 622 votes, beating Paul Brown, who received 387 votes. Tan beat Brown at the University Center polling station by more than 80 votes and at the McCarthy Hall site by more than 160 votes.

"I'm surprised that this many people voted because it seemed like not very many people turned out," Tan said. "It's good that I won, but it's also very important for the people who voted for me that I win.

"People say AS has become so much politics," said Tan, a member of the Cambodian Students Association. "I hope to help bring down the politics and the backstabbing that people do to each other."

Motala, who is from the School of Engineering and Computer Science, said he and Tan will "work toward a more diversified AS. This is definitely a new beginning for AS."

Brown, who has openly joked with Tan throughout the election, said that if anyone else besides himself had to be elected, he would have wanted that person to be Tan.

"There he is, sitting in the captain's chair," Brown said referring to Tan. "My professor will be very happy to know that I can do research next year," instead of attending to AS duties, said Brown, a graduate student.

Former presidential candidate John Armstrong, who was disqualified for re-

See RUNOFF, Page 3

Tan's surprise win was prominently featured in CSUF's campus newspaper, The Daily Titan.

addition, I didn't share the same views as the Greek system, and I wasn't willing to be a Greek "puppet" or lose my proud identity as a Cambodian American.

Don't count on "block" votes. Since I couldn't rely on any automatic votes, I had to focus on grassroots campaigning in the College of Business. I spoke at more than 30 classes and student organization meetings and relied on friends to pass out flyers. Running on a theme of eliminating overcrowding, I overcame my public speaking phobia and defeated three other candidates, including the hand-picked Greek choice. It was the first time in memory that the winning Board of Directors candidate was not endorsed by the Greeks.

The run for the presidency. After serving an uneventful but highly educational year as a board member, and no longer a political novice, I still saw a lack of diversity in student government. While there were a few board members like myself who spoke on behalf of minorities, we ultimately lacked the votes to give minority groups their share of the "pie."

After a meeting in spring 1991, fellow Finance Committee members and I began talking about the upcoming ASI presidential election. Someone commented about how wide-open the field was and Yusuf Motala, a fellow committee and board member, turned to me and jokingly said, "Hey, maybe we should run. We can win it." I, of course, laughed at the thought. Hearing Yusuf's remarks, another committee member said, "Look at those clowns thinking of running." Neither Yusuf nor I believed the idea was so absurd after we heard this. For one, our collective student government experience was comparable to other candidates.'

While the thought of running soon faded for me, it didn't leave Yusuf's mind so quickly. Later that evening, an hour before the deadline to submit a candidate application, Yusuf came over with the form in hand, saying, "Let's do it." Though I thought he was crazy at the time, I said "sure."

We then had a decision to make. Who was going to be president? Without any thorough process, we decided that I would run for president, since I had slightly more ASI experience. After serving a year as a board member, I had established a strong reputation as a fighter and a voice for minorities, while Yusuf was active, popular, and well-known. We complemented each other well.

Which groups will support you? We estimated that as minorities ourselves, we would perhaps get as much as 85 to 90 percent of Latino and African-American votes. We had a very small on-campus population, so dorm residents weren't a powerful voting block. Even though Yusuf was active in a residence hall organization, we didn't spend a great deal of time speaking to dorm residents or groups. For me, it was Asian, Latino, and African-American students who would be our voters.

Speak, speak, speak. Before and during election days, Yusuf and I spoke to classes and student organizations. A close friend went class to class, calling and writing the professors beforehand to ask if I could have three to five minutes. My opponents didn't do this. While I spoke to about 30 classes and clubs, my opponents maybe did five. I even spoke to Greek councils. Knowing very well that the Greeks would support fellow Greeks, I still went to speak to them. It was a scary moment — many of them had this suspicious, "What's this Asian guy doing here" look on their faces. I wanted to show them I wasn't going to concede anything, even though I knew that I wasn't going to get a single vote from them.

I had several key volunteers who devoted as much time to the campaign as I did, because they believed in Yusuf and me and what we represented. There was a secondary level of 20 to 25 students who gave me a few hours on a certain day. I created a schedule so that if one person left the polls, we would have someone to replace him or her. I knew who was supposed to come in, where they would be positioned, and how long they would be there.

Our campaign theme was "Diversity Brings Unity." My most important issue was to promote equal input from various minority groups and proportional funding. During my presidency, we were able to increase funding for minority programs substantially.

Don't sweat debates or endorsements. We had one debate, which was more for *The Daily Titan* campus newspaper than for the audience of about 100 supporters. The paper didn't endorse anyone, but I felt like their coverage of the campaign was pro-Greek. Most of the top editors were Greek, and the slant of some articles favored Greeks, we felt. They weren't blatant lies, but they were biased.

Luckily, there wasn't any dirt for them to drag up on me. While I was a silent figure, a lot of people respected me. They knew I was unwilling to compromise my beliefs. Because there was a lot of backstabbing in the previous administration, we wanted to restore ASI's good image.

Don't spend too much time on flyers. With a campaign spending limit of $150, we couldn't do newspaper ads or spend a lot for shirts or buttons, so we focused on producing inexpensive, simple flyers that our volunteers could post and hand out. We asked friends to help, gave them staple guns, and had them put up posters in 10 campus buildings.

Some of our flyers were printed in different colors, including white to represent Caucasians, black to represent African-Americans, yellow to represent Asians, and brown to represent Latinos.

Election day. We had volunteers stationed around each of the

Political games characterize AS elections during 1990-91

By Joe McDonald
Daily Titan

They all said that they wanted a clean campaign throughout election week.

But after numerous violations and hearings from the elections and judicial commissions which resulted in candidate John Armstrong's disqualification, Vitthara Tan won the Associated Students' presidency for the 1991-92 academic year in a runoff election against Paul Brown.

Although Armstrong had the endorsement of the Inter-Fraternity Council and Brown had the Panhellenic Council's endorsement, Tan was victorious in an election normally won by the candidate with the strongest Greek support.

Armstrong, who received the most votes in the first election, was disqualified on the second day the polls were open after the Elections Commission found him guilty of repeated campaign violations.

Armstrong was reprimanded after Bob Ford, a community service officer, and a Delta Sigma Phi fraternity brother of Armstrong, removed fliers from posting areas, a violation of AS elections code, according to Ken Stewart, chariman of the Elections Commission.

As a result of the violation, Armstrong was to remove all of his campaign fliers from all posting areas by 8:45 a.m. the next day. After the deadline passed, election commissioners said

Vitthara Tan

Joe Ahn

they removed more than 400 of his fliers from campus posting areas.

The commission met after they removed all the fliers and voted to disqualify Armstrong, Stewart said.

Because no candidate received a majority of the votes in the first election, Armstrong would have run off against Tan in the second election if he had

not been disqualified.

But Brown, who finished third, ran against Tan despite Armstrong's efforts to disqualify Brown, a graduate teaching assistant, for being a Cal State Fullerton faculty member.

"Vitthara and I have suffered a severe disadvantage," Armstrong said at the elections commissions hearing at which he filed a complaint against Brown. "Just as a part-time student who is a coach (with the Athletic Department) could not run for AS office, neither can Brown."

The elections commission said Paul Brown was not a CSUF faculty member and, as a result, could participate in the election.

Had Armstrong not won the endorsement of the IFC, current AS President Joe Ahn would have rerun for the presidency after a year in which two members of his executive cabinet left on bad terms with him during the middle of the year.

Elisha Back,. former vice president of finance, was dismissed by the AS board on Feb. 12. Although Ahn said she did not fulfill her AS responsibilities, many people within AS ·

Both Back and Ahn said they shared a· poor working relationship with each other the day she was dismissed.

Lloyd Kerr, former vice president of administration after April 9, said he resigned after watching Ahn "railroad Elisha Back without consulting the rest of his executive cabinet concerning her job performance.

four polling places to hand out flyers from the time the poll opened until it closed. We weren't allowed to campaign closer than 50 feet from the polls -— the elections coordinators even had a tape measure out to make sure we weren't closer. Our people stood right next to the tape.

While our opponents had volunteers there, they only showed

for an hour or two. For sheer consistency and dedication, we definitely outmatched them. It was the first time that anyone deployed that kind of intense campaigning.

Sometimes you need a little luck. Despite this organization, our big break came when the Greek system couldn't agree on a single presidential candidate. This indecision immediately became a huge advantage for us, because it meant the Greek vote would be divided.

In the general election, no candidate managed to get a majority of the 1,500 votes cast out of 25,000 students (or 6 percent). Turnout was comparable with previous years. The candidate receiving the highest number got about 450 votes, while I got 420 votes for second place. The first-place candidate was supported by fraternity houses, while the third-place candidate had the support of sororities.

The campaign got ugly soon after the first election when the first-place candidate was disqualified for tearing down campaign flyers. As a result, we went into the runoff election a week later against the third-place candidate.

In protest, fraternity members refused to vote for the third-place candidate in the runoff. In fact, they didn't even turn out to vote. With half of the automatic Greek vote gone, we won the runoff by about 200 votes, with a much lower overall turnout because students were losing interest.

After watching the votes being tabulated and then getting the unofficial results, I remember being physically exhausted and mentally burned out. While I thought I had a chance to win all along, it kind of surprised me when I actually did. I remember getting this sinking feeling: "Now what? What have I done?"

Because school was my number-one priority, I didn't skip classes or miss any tests during the campaign. I've always been good in school, so I haven't needed to study as much as some students do. Once I was elected, however, I did take a lighter class load, so I had more time to devote to my presidential duties. Instead of 15 credits, I took six, for example. When I graduated, I had earned a solid 3.4 GPA.

After my term of office, we left a legacy of offering more money to minority groups and disproved some misconceptions about minority programs. I think we demonstrated that minority issues are as legitimate as anyone's. Since I left office, the heightened funding has continued to be stable. Unfortunately, minority representation has declined since I left office.

Two years after I was gone, *The Daily Titan* was still writing about my ethical standards as a model use of power. We were very highly respected, probably one of the best administrations CSUF ever had as far as ethics. We promised to bring legitimacy to ASI and we did.

Many factors contribute to a win. In summary, I needed organization, a few reliable and hardworking friends who were willing to go all out, and a general understanding of how student government is run. I also needed to know who the "players" were, to assess my potential voter base, and to choose legitimate issues that students care about. And lastly, I really needed a little luck, too.

One could easily argue that I won my race for the presidency because of chance or destiny, even though I did employ some skillful campaign strategies. But there were many factors which contributed to my becoming student body president, and the absence of any of them could have led to my defeat. My victory really does prove that an underdog should never give up, even on a campus where a few seem to dominate the political landscape.

Contact: Vitthara Tan
Address: c/o EOP Admissions,
California State University, Fullerton,
800 N. State College Blvd., Fullerton, CA 92831

An Average "Joe" Wins at San Diego State University

By Joe Horiye
1990-91 Associated Students President
San Diego State University, California

Introduction

Horiye, 28, served as 1990-91 A.S. president at San Diego State University (SDSU). In addition to his duties as president, he was actively involved in the Asian Pacific Student Alliance, Rotaract, and Theta Chi fraternity.

After graduating in 1992 with a degree in business administration finance, Horiye now is special projects director for the San Diego Community Housing Corporation.

How Horiye United Diverse Groups In a Landslide Election

My journey to become student body president at SDSU made me understand the terms "Respect, Responsibility, Resourcefulness, Resiliency, and Risk." What I remember most about my election isn't my opposition, speeches, or flyers — it's the overwhelming support I received from groups and individuals, strangers and friends.

I decided to run for Associated Students president toward the end of my term as the A.S. vice president of finance. I had achieved my goals, which included more financial assistance for students and funding for groups. But I also realized that more needed to be done. Simply put, I wanted to make a difference. My sense of commitment in assisting others was inspired by my own past hardships and experiences having grown up in a rough neighborhood. My mentors helped others without expecting anything in return. These reasons inspired me to seek the office.

With 35,000 students, SDSU has the largest enrollment in the California State University system. Student leaders and groups compete annually for control of Associated Students. Because the stakes are high, the competition is fierce. I found that the best way to overcome my reservations about running was to surround myself with people who would support me from beginning to end, win or lose; quality people respected for their honesty, integrity, and judgment.

Assess your chances before you run. The first step was to analyze the feasibility of running based on my past experiences and future prospects. I had run a similar campaign to become v.p. of finance and was in charge of the $7.3 million A.S. budget. I talked with the current president, other A.S. leaders, students, employees, and administrators to get their feedback on my chances of winning. They were supportive overall.

I also built an extensive, diverse support base. This included strong associations with the Interfraternity and Panhellenic Greek system, ethnic groups, honor societies, business organizations, and students with no organizational affiliation. I was an active member of several groups, not just a member in name only.

To build this support base, I had to motivate others. This is something I did by investing time and effort into developing relationships that were genuine and real. Relationship building meant more to me than just being mere social acquaintances or "colleagues while campaigning." It meant taking the time to get to know the person and letting them know that I would actively support him or her. Just as respect is earned over time, our best relationships and friendships are also developed over time.

And there were other issues. If elected, I would be the first Asian Pacific Islander to serve as student body president. Because I had support from both sides, I also would be the first candidate in some time to have a real chance of strengthening communication between two of the most influential, yet traditionally divisive special interests groups on campus — the Greek system and the minority organizations. My background included service as a member of both groups, so I understood their needs and concerns.

I had two opponents. Both candidates had strong backing from ethnic groups and business organizations. In fact, we knew that we would split the support bases; however, no one knew exactly where the lines would be drawn.

Find volunteers you trust. The next step was to form a management team. I recruited nine students who I trusted to give me objective analysis and constructive criticism. This team functioned as the campaign Board of Directors. The Board's responsibilities included campaign bylaw compliance, financial management, graphic design, volunteer scheduling, marketing, and materials production. There was always a distinct separation of duties for the team members, including myself. The alternative was to have a single campaign manager coordinate the effort.

I preferred the board style because the team members shared responsibility. Specific tasks were assigned to members based on their interests and expertise. All members were responsible for brainstorming ideas to be incorporated to the development of the overall strategy. My role was to serve as the chair, with the authority to exercise final approval. Meetings were scheduled for regular progress updates.

My platform issues were based on concerns from meeting with other students and campus leaders. I wanted to represent their ideas and use my coalition-building strengths and problem-solving skills to work on developing real solutions. These included reducing student fees, providing more student loans, enhancing communication among the different special-interest groups, supporting campus development, and ensuring that students were informed about services and programs available to them. On a side note, I recall the biggest obstacle was actually convincing my fellow students that they had a real stake and voice in the system.

Know the campaign rules. Next, it's very important to get immediate clarification on all election guidelines before the campaign begins. I can't stress this next point enough. For example, you can't do "phone banking" — making calls to potential voters who live more than a one-mile radius from campus, and you can't campaign within 100 feet of a polling

Joe Horiye used large wooden signs around campus and had a central information table to generate interest in his campaign for A.S. presidency.

booth. I saw different interpretations on the same regulation that resulted in the immediate disqualification of several candidates. The bottom line is that you have to understand the rules and if you choose not to, you must be willing to accept ultimate responsibility for your decisions.

One of the campus election code guidelines, the maximum $275 spending limit, forced my team to make some hard choices. Knowing that sometimes there is campaign sabotage, we tried to account for materials such as large, expensive signs that might get destroyed. In the past, some candidates neglected to include replacement costs in their original budgets and they ran out of materials during the campaign. Fortunately, we didn't have to deal with that problem, but you should budget for replacement materials just to be safe.

With a budget of only $275, we couldn't afford to run any ads in the campus newspaper, *The Daily Aztec*. Occasionally, other campaigns ran ads in the personal classifieds section, but we decided to use our money elsewhere. Knowing that our campus was too large to post signs everywhere, we budgeted for 1,000 sticker buttons, three large wood signs, and some miscellaneous items, with the remainder to be spent solely on flyers.

In-kind donations weren't allowed. The campaign rules did

permit us to accept used donated materials, such as paint brushes, wood, and supplies which were accounted for and included in the budget at depreciated values.

We identified the areas with the most foot traffic and put signs there. We made sure that the signs were visible at nearby voting booths. The rest of campus we blanketed with flyers and volunteers. We used half-sheet flyers instead of full sheets because the same message is communicated and you get double the quantity at the same price.

Ask for club endorsements. The two weeks of A.S. elections are divided into two phases. The first week concentrates on getting endorsements from organizations and clubs, while the second week concentrates on actually getting students to the polls. All of the major voting blocks, including the Greek system, the minority groups, the college councils, and the Residence Hall Association, participate. All of the candidates typically attend a group meeting, present their platforms and answer questions. Later the group will vote on who to endorse.

The Daily Aztec didn't endorse me, and because not all of the press was always positive, my friends hid the campus newspaper so that I wouldn't read it and get more stressed.

Winning the support of major clubs and organizations can help boost the morale of your campaign staff, but don't assume that this means guaranteed votes at the polls. It's best to accept invitations from all individual organizations, even though you may have the support of their larger system or association. You may get the Interfraternity Council to endorse you, but that doesn't mean the individual houses will also. At SDSU, most student groups accommodate the candidates to hear their views if you contact the club president and get permission in advance.

One tangible benefit of getting endorsements is that organizations that sponsor you can make up campaign materials on your behalf, as long as it's in a normally scheduled publication or announcement, such as a flyer or newsletter. These expenses are exempted from the spending limit.

To put it mildly, stress levels were at an all-time high during the second week of campaigning. This is when your fellow students will either support your platform, disagree with it, or just not care at all. SDSU elections last for five days, and historically, voting trends indicate that the two heaviest voting periods are the first two days and the last day, with organizations choosing to vote earlier in the process and individuals casting their votes at the end of the week.

During the second week, more than 250 supporters rallied behind me from dawn to dusk to hand out flyers, to encourage their friends to vote, to stand up in their classrooms and make announcements, and more importantly, to just believe in me and be by my side. I believe this "small army" of volunteers was a testament to my ability to motivate people and effectively communicate and share my vision. The excitement that was created motivated and inspired others to join the team. Each volunteer had a role to play in this campaign. In fact, at the end of the elections, most of my supporters were still out there, standing next to me in the pouring rain.

My supporters' commitment and strength amazes me to this day. No pun intended, but I was just an "average Joe." I didn't rely on flashy flyers or even a slogan. I just tried to be as professional, yet as personal as possible. Simply put, I was just myself.

There are two additional points that I remember well from those 14 days. I remember being the first one awake and the last one to go to sleep. I also recall that I had something to do every minute of the day, whether it was passing out flyers, giving speeches, or fine tuning a strategy meeting.

I remember receiving death threats — anonymous prank phone calls threatening my life if I ran. Some candidates also have had their homes vandalized during campaigns. Whoever made these calls was trying to intimidate me, but it didn't work.

Even if my opponents didn't have a lot in common with me before the election, we certainly did by the end. All three of us understood the pressures of a college campaign, and I believe when it was over, we had earned each other's grudging respect.

The voter turn out for Spring 1990 elections was 11.76

percent of the student population. When the ballots were finally tallied, I got 64 percent or 2,521 votes. My nearest challenger won 780 votes. The results are announced around midnight in the Aztec Center, our student union. The candidates and supporters congregate near the AS office, waiting for the vote totals to be displayed on a large chalkboard. The results are written on one side, then it's flipped over dramatically for everyone to see. Because it was so packed in there, I couldn't see the board and didn't even realize that I had won until I was carried out of the room on the shoulders of strangers and friends. That moment is what I remember most.

I would like to believe that I won because I was the best person for the position. And I would like to believe that I won because of my personality, strong grassroots networks, and issues. But the bottom line is that the students of SDSU validated my efforts through their votes. Winning a student position is not only based on name recognition, popularity or experience. It is being able to win the support from your peers, and I'm forever grateful.

Looking back, my student leadership days are marked with both tremendous honor and great humility. In the end, what's often overlooked is this: when you run for office, it's not only your integrity on trial, but your supporters' as well. With that said, let me also stress that while becoming student body president was a tremendous achievement in my undergraduate career, my greatest accomplishment was earning my diploma. And as a "Yonsei" (fourth generation American of Japanese ancestry) I became the first in my family to graduate from college, and also became the first American of Asian Pacific Islander ancestry to become A.S. president at SDSU. As a former student leader, I can tell you that education is the real reason why we come to college.

Contact: Joe Horiye
Address: 8799 Balboa Ave., #100,
San Diego, CA 92123
Phone: (619) 620-2519
Fax: (619) 292-4532

The First African American SGA President At Virginia Tech

By Ronnie E. Stephenson
1993-94 Student Government Association President
Virginia Tech

Introduction

Stephenson, 24, was 1993-94 Student Government Association president at Virginia Tech, a public university with an enrollment of 24,000. He was the first sophomore and first African American to serve as president.

Stephenson also was an orientation leader, served on several city committees, and on the University Council. Stephenson currently is working in congressional affairs.

How Stephenson Battled the Odds to Win at Virginia Tech

If you think that college elections aren't vicious, I can tell you that during my campaign I battled major deception, vigorous attacks, dishonesty, and tyranny by the students running SGA and the candidates chosen to follow in their footsteps.

Before running for SGA president, I ran for Class of 1995 president. I viewed this as the perfect way to help me become more active on campus. This experience would later prove useful to me because of the organizational knowledge and skills I gained. This race was against two other candidates supported by large organizations. Since I wasn't a member of a fraternity or a large campus group, I rounded up new friends who helped organize my campaign. A lot of the first-year students were eager to help.

I recruited some volunteers from the debates we had during classes, which was a first. My opponents and I picked classes with the largest audience, usually more than 300 students, then asked teachers to give us a few minutes before and during class. Individually, I also reached out to other students by speaking in a lot of smaller classes, and also had friends and campaign helpers speak in theirs.

Spending limits for campus campaigns were about $100. My two opponents had the advantage of having their costs absorbed by their fraternities. I didn't have money coming in from any group, nor did I have funds of my own to contribute. Luckily, I convinced a new copying business to give me a good price on large quantities of flyers, and friends donated other materials and resources.

Right before the Freshmen Class election, I signed up volunteers to stand at the voting booths and hold signs. I also had signs that read, "Plain and Simple. No Balloons. No Gimmicks. Vote Ronnie E. Stephenson for President!" I knew that my opponents would try to create attention by using balloons, candy, and other campaign tricks that had become a tradition at our school. And after campaigning for one and a half weeks, I won.

Get educated before you run. After winning, I scheduled meetings with university officials and began to develop an understanding of the history of the university, the town, student organizations, and the class system. Because of this "informal education" in the various departments and functions of the university, I had become an information source for many people who couldn't find answers anywhere else. I became the person that organizations turned to for help, encouragement, and advice. Students began to discuss my name with running for higher office because of this knowledge base.

But it wasn't until winter break that I started thinking seriously about running for SGA president. The feedback on whether I should run was mixed — most of my friends encouraged me, but those within SGA felt that, as a sophomore, I should wait. Never before had anyone held an executive office or even run as a sophomore, nor had any candidate ever won without being part of a fraternity or sorority. Finally I decided to run when it was clear that the objections weren't based on my qualifications, but on my

Putting service first

By PAUL DELLINGER
STAFF WRITER

The president of Tech's student government brings plenty of ideas to office with him

BLACKSBURG — Ronnie E. Stephenson can be credited with a couple of firsts as he starts his junior year at Virginia Tech.

As the new president of its Student Government Association, Stephenson, 20, is the first student not a senior as well as the first black to win that position. All the other officers are seniors.

He grins at the thought of running again and winning the post in his senior year, but he has been too busy to think of that right now.

"I have no idea," he said. "Honestly, I can't say. We'll see when that time approaches."

But being a two-term president wouldn't be a first. Another student, who attended Tech for five years, served twice.

Of course, Stephenson laughed, he could stay five years and try for three terms, but quickly added that he will be gone at the end of his fourth year to attend law school.

SGA candidates run during the spring semester, and spend 2½ weeks in a university-wide campaign. Stephenson thrived on it.

"Politics is something you can enjoy. It's not all evil and deceitful and cruel . . . as many people perceive it to be," he said.

"That's what I aspire to do later on is public service, preferably on the national level," he said.

Stephenson already has mastered the political science of acronyms.

To provide information to students 24 hours a day on everything from bus schedules to meeting times, he and the other officers have started "SNAP" — the Student News Automated Phone-line.

They ran on a platform called "Students FIRST" — Forever Interested in Restoring Student Trust.

Stephenson got lots of media attention after becoming the first African American SGA president in Virginia Tech's history.

year in school.

SGA candidates usually ran on a ticket with candidates for president, vice president, treasurer, and secretary which allows large groups to form voting "blocks", and make it difficult for individual students and organizations, or small groups to win.

But the rules changed during my campaign. Students were still allowed to run as a group, but they were no longer recognized on ballots by their ticket name. The rule change was intended to make it easier for more independent students to get involved with Student Government.

About a week before the deadline to file for candidacy, we learned that our secretary candidate was not eligible to run, because of some new rules we weren't aware of. After lobbying on his behalf without success, I had to give in and choose another candidate.

Then I was informed that two of our four candidates weren't

eligible. Our opponents objected to the filing deadline extension we had been given, so the elections chair reversed her ruling. We protested, a hearing was held, with the result being our candidates could still run, but one candidate's name wouldn't appear on the ballot.

Once we were eligible to run, we set up a campaign committee — a smaller "core" group to help brainstorm and another larger group to recruit new volunteers and create banners, signs, and flyers. The brainstorming committee developed a campaign theme and ticket name, F.I.R.S.T (Forever Interested in Restoring Student Trust). I added "Students" and our name became "Students FIRST."

The brainstorming committee then started scheduling speaking engagements at all possible organizations and classes. I told them that no group or class was too small and that no organization should be excluded because of its support for the other ticket.

We also developed our campaign platform. In the past, most candidates either had good ideas without offering solutions or some even had flaky ideas such as installing beer machines on campus and having block parties in residence halls. So we developed a platform that identified three target areas. One was better communication — I wanted SGA to be a viable resource for every student, and I wanted students to be aware of how they could get involved in SGA.

The second issue was improved campus safety. After talking to students, the university police, and town officials, we proposed that more buses should run at night from main locations like the library, since about 15,000 students live off campus and travel to classes using our free bus system. We also noted that many residence halls were unsecured at night, and thus open for strangers to wander through.

The third area addressed other issues. First was my commitment to the environment — I wanted to make conserving money and resources through more efficient management a priority. The second issue dealt with the fund distribution board for student organizations. Finally, we wanted to build greater school spirit by sponsoring events such as bus trips to away football games. At Virginia Tech, only two weeks are allowed for campaigning, and each candidate is allowed to spend $200. We also provided an itemized expense record, including receipts.

We spent the first week of campaigning putting up flyers, speaking to groups and classes, and putting up three 3' by 5' banners at the student union building and two other heavily traveled areas. Made from white sheets donated to us by hotels, the banners were painted with waterproof paint. As election day neared, we moved two banners closer to the dining halls to attract on-campus students as they were going to dinner.

Obey the poster rules. To cut down on litter, only one poster per candidate could appear on each bulletin board across campus. We printed about 1,000 flyers each, and plastered the campus as much as we were allowed, including bathroom and hall doors in the residence halls and in the lounges. We weren't allowed to put them on dorm doors without the permission of the residents, nor were we permitted to slide them under doors.

Our strategy was to hang posters early in the campaign's first week so students would quickly get to know us. Then we systematically replaced posters that were torn down or covered over.

Speak to lots of classes. While putting up posters was important, I was convinced that our most important campaign strategy would be to speak to as many classes as possible to get our message out. Our speaking schedule was horrendous. After speaking all day between our own classes, we attended as many as five "7 p.m." club and organization meetings every night. Thanks to a lot of advance work by volunteers, we had the exact locations and traveling route mapped out on a chart. Also to avoid conflicting meetings, we asked each group's leaders to set a time for us, so we could stagger the times of our visits and make it to all of the meetings.

Even though we tailored the presentation to the group, our principal message never changed. Our greatest test came during appearances before organizations that our opponents belonged to — we knew they would not and could not support our ticket. Some

Stephenson organized and spoke at a rally against tuition increases that was attended by several hundred students and was covered extensively by local and statewide media.

of my volunteers wondered why I would even waste time on them, but I looked forward to it. It proved that our ticket was willing to reach out to everyone, even our opponents, which spoke volumes about our character. I later learned that we got quite a bit of silent support from many members of those groups.

It's important to note that our opponents were good at campaigning — their problem was overconfidence and a bit of arrogance. They knew they had the inside track and had the support of four large organizations, including a couple of the larger fraternities and sororities and the Corps Cadets, made up of then about 500 students, who live, eat, and do just about every-thing together. They even march to dinner together.

Knowing this, they refused to debate us. They also asked that we not sit in on their presentations to organizations. Rather than play dirty, we respected their request.

In the final week, we unveiled a new idea — a commercial featuring each of us giving a short speech. It took five hours to complete the actual taping, then it was edited, and music was added. The final commercial was three minutes long, which we then recorded continuously on two 20-minute tapes. Then, after getting permission, we aired the spots at two different locations in our student union for an entire day.

They were created by a student not in our campaign using professional editing equipment and cost us about $50. I don't know how effective it was, but they were a lot of fun to make and it infuriated our opponents and their allies, who were mad because we had a new idea and they didn't have time to do one of their own.

During the last week, our opponents invested a lot of time trying to solicit votes from off-campus students. They hung banners from apartments and other off-campus buildings, and also made buttons and hand stamps with their ticket name.

Focus on the most likely voters. Our strategy didn't emphasize off-campus campaigning because we knew that the most likely voters were students who had seen our presentations in classes or at club meetings. Also, we knew that off-campus students rarely go to the main parts of campus, such as dining halls, so voting tends to be inconvenient for them. Which brings me to our last great campaign initiative.

Several days before the election, we did something that had never been done before — we had postcards made. Using regular paper printed on both sides, we cut the sheets into four cards per page. Knowing that 8,800 students live on campus, we knew there were 4,400 dorm rooms. Two days before election day, we stayed up all night sorting these cards into bundles that matched the exact number of rooms in each residence hall. The cards were then rubber-banded together with the name of the residence hall labeled across each stack of cards. Then we took them to the campus postal service at around 6:30 a.m. the day before the election. Our hope was that most students would get these cards the day before the election and make a mental note of the event. We knew they would get it no later than election day, which was perfect to remind them to vote and vote for us.

The cards were simple — one side was addressed generically and included our ticket name. The reverse side featured our individual names and positions, along with just a reminder to vote. Election day was rainy and cold. Instead of having the voting booth outdoors as they usually are, they were moved inside nearby buildings. When it rains, students take different routes to get to class, and having the polls inside, meant they weren't as visible. Students were less likely to vote as a result.

Each ticket was allowed to have two people holding official campaign material at the voting booths. Fortunately, our supporters weathered the rain to hold signs and pass out literature.

At 7 p.m. the polls closed — we wouldn't know the outcome until the next day. We had no exit polls and now way of knowing how close we were. We did know that the other ticket was beginning to show signs of doubt — they were filing protests right and left, questioning every aspect of our campaign. They complained that we sent postcards to everyone on campus, even though it was perfectly legal.

The next morning, I got a call announcing our victory. There's no doubt that the rain hurt us — we had predicted that if the day was nice we would have likely seen a record turnout.

I think our ticket appealed to a lot of students because of the sincerity of our issues. Our presentations seemed to be real, whereas the other ticket seemed as if they were reading from a script. We were accessible — we even ate together as a ticket and joined any available group in the dining halls. We had a plan and the students could sense our commitment to meeting those goals.

Although we never spoke negatively of our opponents unless questioned about their policies, the fact that they would not even debate us or allow us to see and hear their campaign rhetoric was an indication of their weakness, elitism, and lack of openness and frankness that many students appreciated from our campaign.

Contact: Ronnie E. Stephenson
Address: 20 Fields Dr., Hampton, VA 23664-1771
Phone: (757) 851-6230

A Two-Vote Victory Margin At Albertson College of Idaho

By *Jennifer Vroman*
1996-97 Associated Students President
Albertson College of Idaho

Introduction

Vroman, 22, focuses her campus involvement on presidential duties, her work as a resident assistant, and classes.

After graduating in May 1997 with a degree in business administration, she plans to work in employee development and training.

How Vroman Won At A Small College

It wasn't until March 1996 that I decided to run for student body president. I had been thinking since fall 1995 that I could make a difference, get more involved, and have fun during my senior year. I was a junior and had been the Outdoor Program Director during my sophomore year, an ACI senator for almost two years and a member of various other campus, faculty, and Board of Trustees committees. I had won the Abbott Award as the outstanding woman junior, was named outstanding senator, and was completing my first year as a resident assistant. I probably was one of the most active students on campus.

Although numbering only about 30 members, the Associated Student Government at Albertson College of Idaho (ACI) is usually comprised of dedicated, determined, and highly involved students. Located in Caldwell, ACI is a private liberal arts college with 650 students.

Our elections are held right after spring break, usually around the first of May. I kept the fact that I was running for president very low profile until I knew who my competition would be. Typically, everyone waits until the last day to submit a declaration. My competition was two other juniors and a freshman — all male. I was excited at the prospect of a challenging race. Most of the women students thought I probably would win, and I think I was the favorite in the general election. The freshman opponent was very outspoken and ran on his ties with the Idaho legislature, while my top opponent was the yearbook editor. The other candidate was a junior who was well-liked and strong academically, but hadn't served in any leadership positions on campus.

When I returned after spring break, one of my opponents already had put up signs. I'm fortunate that my best friend happens to be a whiz on the computer, so the first thing we did was create four 8 1/2" by 11" flyer designs and then make about 120 copies to hang around campus. There really aren't any restrictions on where we can put up posters, except for windows in the performing arts building and on the library doors.

Come up with clever posters. I decided to campaign using my last name as a focus since it would easily separate me from the other candidates, whose names were Bonine, Cafferty, and Ellsworth. My grandpa came up with a slogan I used on my most popular sign: "First there was Spiderman, then there was Superman, Now there's VROMAN." By superimposing my head on top of a Wonder Woman body found on the Internet and copying the signs onto fuchsia paper, we not only gave voters something catchy to remember but also something to laugh about.

My other popular sign was designed by my sister, who helped me while she was on spring break from high school. We utilized the "V" in my name as a check mark. On the posters, we drew a box around the "V" to give the impression of a vote. On all my signs, I made sure that my name and the office I was seeking were included. We didn't include the date of the election, because it's promoted already by the current AS vice president, who's in charge of the elections.

I concentrated my postering efforts on the residence halls

and the academic buildings. About half of the student body lives on campus, and this group has a much higher voter turnout than off-campus students.

Be visible. During election week I made myself available everywhere. I ate in the cafeteria for all meals (normally I didn't hang out there), sat in the Student Union Building between classes, and spoke to every person I met. I didn't need to speak to classes or group meetings because of our school's small size.

FIRST THERE WAS SPIDERMAN
THEN THERE WAS SUPERMAN

NOW THERE'S VROMAN!!!!

Jen for ASACI President

Our debate, "Elections Speech Night," is traditionally a sparsely attended event, but this year the lecture hall filled up. Since there were so many candidates, everyone brought their friends and their "group." I was definitely nervous — we only had five minutes for our prepared speeches and then had to answer about 10 randomly selected questions from the crowd. The presidential candidates give their speeches last. Since we spoke in alphabetical order, this gave me a definite advantage — a chance to improvise and respond to comments made by my opponents.

In my speech, I focused on three important campus issues: the need for tradition, such as focusing more on homecoming and the finals breakfast; improving college and community relations, so that businesses would offer internships and recruit students; and offering more activities for students, such as bonfires, movies, dances, and entertainers.

I also emphasized that I was a hard worker and had experience with the student senate, the Board of Trustees, and the administration. Most importantly, I lived on campus and planned to do so the following year. I also promised to continue to be on the meal plan. By illustrating these key points, I felt that I could relate to students and their concerns. If I was eating the cafeteria food, I could say, "I feel your pain." The other candidates had lived on campus, but weren't planning to in the future.

Speech Night always concludes with a question from the outgoing student body president, and much to my surprise, he asked us the same question I had asked him as a student a year earlier: "Next year, when you're sitting in the audience, what as student body president would like to have achieved in the past year?" I said I'd like to know that I made the college experience better for at least one student. Then I'd know that I had done my job.

I found that during the question-and-answer period, it was best to keep my answers short yet sincere. I didn't try to make promises or guarantees on the spur of the moment. I did have a list from an earlier brainstorming session to reference if someone asked a very specific question.

Our monthly campus newspaper, *The Coyote*, covered the election after the fact, so there was no pre-election or debate coverage. The paper really doesn't influence elections or endorse candidates either.

Campaign door-to-door. At 3 a.m. the night before the election, I stuck a "Vote Vroman" piece of paper on every campus door. I recruited friends to help, so it only took about an hour. This last-minute strategy worked. In the general election, I won with 37.1 percent, with the next highest total at 26.8 percent. We had a 56.7 percent total voter turnout campus-wide. Since the race was split four ways, no candidate received 50.1 percent, so we had a runoff. Because of scheduling

Vroman

ASACI President

difficulties, the second election was held five days later.

During the runoff, my opponent beat me to the punch with a door-to-door campaign with posters that said, "Get rid of your headache and vote Cafferty." He attached a sample of Tylenol to every poster. I had a similar plan — my faithful and resourceful friends drove to the 24-hour grocery store and copy shop and made signs which read "Don't be suckered by the competition....Jen Vroman President." To each sign we attached a sucker, then put them up on doors. When residents woke up in the morning, they were greeted with a treat, and I saw lots of them eating the suckers later that day.

This strategy is pretty common at our school. The year before, a candidate named Cherry cut out signs in the shape of a cherry with rounded stems to slip over door handles.

During election day, the poll in the Union is open from 9 a.m. to 8 p.m. I was determined to get every person I knew to vote. I sat around figuring up what votes I thought I could count on, but I really didn't determine exactly how many votes I would need. I was worried that getting too mathematical might take away from the campaign.

I was constantly reminding students to get out and vote. Fortunately, many residents on my floor literally walked other students to the voting booth. In the primary election, only 83.6 percent of my building voted. With 60 residents, my building is the second largest on campus. In the runoff, we had 100 percent voter turnout.

After the polls close, the student body vice president and the election board, comprised of a representative from each voting district, tabulate the results. Typically, they call the candidates and then post the results in all of the residence halls and in the Union. I had gone to dinner in Boise, which is about half an hour away, and came back at 9:15 p.m., not expecting the results to be out yet. But I found my friends making a congratulations banner — that's when I freaked out.

Campuswide, voter turnout was 56.9 percent, and I won by a margin of two votes. My political science professor started calling me, in jest, "Landslide Vroman."

Although we don't have campaign spending limitations, I certainly had some personally — I spent under $50 of my own money, which is about what the other candidates spent. At a small school like ACI, money and publicity don't win campaigns. You have to take advantage of the most powerful and accessible resource: students. It's more about who your friends and supporters are and if they're apathetic or will take the initiative to help out and vote. This year, however, there will be a campaign spending limit.

I think my visibility, positive attitude, and willingness to listen to all students — and the fact that I knew lots of freshmen — won me the elections. My job as a resident assistant also contributed, since about half of the total enrollment lives on campus.

By motivating myself, my constituency, and my 25 campaign workers, we ran a campaign free of negativism and apathy and full of enthusiasm and excitement. Fortunately, none of the other candidates played dirty, which is quite a switch from other recent elections.

I also learned how important it is to vote and how much every single vote means, since I won by only two! If I had done any less planning or work, I probably would have lost. This close election taught me to go all out, right up until the last minute, to ensure that I had a chance to win.

Contact: Jennifer Vroman
Address: 2420 Calkins Ave., Idaho Falls, ID 83402
Phone: (208) 459-5508

A "Speaker" Wins at the University of North Dakota

By Tammy Schlinger
1996-97 Student Government President
University of North Dakota

Introduction

Tammy Schlinger, 21, was 1996-97 student body president at the University of North Dakota. In addition to her presidential duties, Schlinger is involved in Mortar Board, Alpha Chi Omega sorority, and the Pi Sigma Alpha honor society.

After graduating in May 1997 with a degree in political science, Schlinger is attending the Syracuse University School of Law.

How Schlinger Used the Personal Touch to Win

As I was deciding to run for president in January 1996, I had no idea just how much work and adventure lay ahead. I wasn't a political novice — I had served as a student senator in 1995 and was involved in the North Dakota Students Association. I knew that I wanted to continue to evolve my role within SG. I was convinced that I had the knowledge, desire, and ability to be an effective president. Most importantly, I had a great deal of pride for UND and was willing to work hard.

My eventual decision to run for president was made knowing I had the support of close friends whose opinions I greatly respected. I also had an outstanding running mate, Kari Gjovik. At UND, the presidential and vice presidential candidates run on the same ticket and are elected together, while the other candidates including senators run on their own. My vice president and I made up the first-ever all-female ticket. This factor added an interesting flair to the campaign.

My running mate and I began by establishing our platform. We knew that we needed to identify issues that were important to the 11,000 UND students. The platform was comprised of some of our personal goals and ideas along with those of our colleagues. The main topics were establishing a 24-hour study facility, increasing Student Government accessibility, attracting more private businesses to campus, and implementing an involvement program known as S.O.A.R (Student Organizations and Activities Recruit). We also talked about the upcoming North Dakota legislative session and the importance of keeping abreast of issues relating to higher education. Some of our platform planks, such as the 24-hour study hall and attracting businesses to set up on campuses, were unique to our campaign. For the record, a Subway restaurant is about to open on campus, and the 24-hour study hall is now in the discussion and early planning stages.

Recruit a core group of volunteers. The next step was to form a campaign committee. We tried to get a broad representation of students — some lived in residence halls and university apartments, others in Greek housing, and some were off-campus students. Our 25 volunteers also were involved in different organizations. While many team members were relatively close friends of mine or my running mate, most didn't know each other.

We then selected a campaign manager to head the committee. My running mate and I chose a student who had been involved in campaigns before. Then we came up with the slogan, "Uniting UND."

We met with the editor of our campus newspaper, *The Dakota Student*, and officially announced our intent to run. There are no limitations on when you can begin campaigning or how far in advance of the March elections you can announce your candidacy.

Don't bank on Greek support. We were one of the first two groups to declare. My chief opponent hadn't been involved in SG, but he was involved in a fraternity. The third-place candidate, also a Greek, had been very involved in SG, having served as a senator and a member of a standing committee. The fourth candidate had

A campaign committee member prepares "Schlinger/Gjovik" banners to hang in key campus locations such as fraternity and sorority houses.

run for state legislature when he was 18 years old.

The year prior to my election, there were only two candidates, one Greek and one independent, so there was solid support from the Greek community for the Greek candidate. However, there are several strong and active groups on campus, so having only Greek support does not guarantee a victory.

We by no means counted on the Greek vote, since there were so many chapters represented by the four candidates and their running mates. We tried to get support from students living in apartments and residence halls, as well as students in clubs and organizations. In fact, we tried hard to avoid catering to Greeks.

Talk to as many groups as possible. In the six-week period between our official announcement and the election, we spoke at two to eight student organization meetings a day. UND has more than 200 campus groups and during the course of the campaign, we were able to meet with about 130 of them. One of our campaign committee members called all the presidents of these groups and set up times for us, then we referred to a master schedule. At some group meetings, we had a time limit, while others were more laid back. Sometimes our opponents were there, but not always.

Traditionally at UND, speaking to groups has been the main way to get support.

Because over 3,000 students live in residence halls, addressing their concerns and getting their support can make a big difference. We also spent a lot of time meeting with hall governments since they have a very active governance system. I had been the programming board chair for the residence halls a few years ago, so I knew about on-campus students' concerns.

When visiting these groups, we discussed our platform issues and answered questions. We also tried to get students to talk about things they would like to see done on campus. Several students had fantastic suggestions — in fact, we came up with our two main campaign issues. Thanks to these meetings, we found it necessary to continually revise our original platform to more accurately meet students' needs.

Taking the time to speak to 130 student groups probably was our biggest key to victory. It wasn't just making speeches though, that did the trick. We took time to answer questions, listen, and try to learn about the needs of each group. I think students sensed our genuine interest which led some of their members to vote for us.

Don't forget flyers. Establishing name recognition was obviously important, so we printed and posted 1,000 campaign flyers with our names and campaign slogan around campus. We also distributed 600 buttons to campaign volunteers who gave them to friends, sorority and fraternity members, and everyone we knew. Yard signs were placed in the lawns of six Greek houses, and "Vote Schlinger/Gjovik" banners were set up at a few fraternity and sorority houses prior to the election. We also spent about $600 on a series of ads in our campus newspaper.

To raise enough money, we sent out letters to many family members and friends. Their generosity helped us to fund the campaign, which cost approximately $1,300. Unlike many schools, UND imposes no limits on campaign spending.

We didn't run radio or T.V. commercials, send out big mailings, or set up a web site. We felt like our signs, buttons, and personal speeches would be adequate. A few days before the election, we set up a table in our student union, the main thorough-fare for off-campus students, with information about our goals and qualifications. Many friends took time out of their schedules to sit at this table to help us gather additional support as election day drew near. A display also was put in a window case in the Union. One opponent also used the window display as a promotional tool.

The campaign proved to be an interesting experience. For six weeks, my running mate and I put our hearts and souls into it. I found myself getting wrapped up in the entire process and spent endless hours campaigning. I learned the importance of both sacrifice and commitment during the process. I know I missed a lot of sleep and didn't have much time for my social life, but I really worked hard not to skip class. There were a few times when the campaign interfered, but classes were still my top priority.

Debates can be good exposure. We had three campus debates, one of which was sponsored by *The Dakota Student*. Held in an open space in the Union, they weren't really debates, but more of a question and answer period. I wish we had had the chance to go at it, but we didn't. Held during the noon hour, about 150 to 200 students attended the first two debates. The third, held in a residence hall, attracted only 50 students from that dorm. I don't know if any students voted for me as a result of these debates, but they were good exposure and were covered in the paper.

The big day arrives. We couldn't campaign on election day at all, which is unusual. Two nights before the election, we took the campus phone directory and had committee members make calls to anyone and everyone. We made at least 5,000 calls that night. While most responses were positive, we did encounter some negative reactions, mainly from the residence halls. Some-times four students share the same suite, but their numbers are listed four times, so some of them got called more than once, which probably was annoying. A few students occasionally would ask "Why should I vote for them? What do they stand for?" Our volunteers would try to answer, but I also did follow-up calls when they wanted more detailed responses. I spent most of my time that night calling my friends and acquaintances to remind them to vote.

The day before the election, which is held the week prior to spring break, *The Dakota Student* endorsed one of our opponents, which wasn't a big surprise. We had prepped our campaign staff knowing that we would have to win it without the paper's endorsement. The editor was a former vice presidential candidate and had been a student senator, so he was not only familiar with SG, but had been very active in it. I think he wanted to see new blood in SG, but I really don't know why the paper's editorial board didn't endorse us.

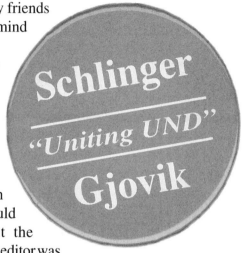

When the election day finally drew near, we got worried that the elections might be canceled. There were forecasts for a blizzard, and we thought that might postpone the election, but fortunately it didn't.

Kari and I won with 888 votes to 822, with 35 percent of the 2,500 ballots cast. The voter turnout was one of the highest in recent memory, mainly because students also were voting on accepting a "plus or minus" grading system. Instead of a 23-percent voter turnout, it usually hovers around 1,800 voters, or 16 percent. So heading into election day, we thought getting 600 to 650 votes would bring us a victory.

After the polls close, every team typically has its own victory party. I was at one of the local hangouts when members of SG came in, grabbed the microphone, and announced the results. Kari and I both were going to give speeches, but I don't remember what I said, as it was just an exciting moment.

To be honest, I don't think anyone was the favorite in this election. No one knew what would happen, and while I was confident, I was by no means sure that I would win. We did know that it would be a close race.

I truly believe that a large part of my campaign's success is a result of the dedication of my friends and the members of the campaign committee. I also think the time we spent visiting with student groups was extremely beneficial, as well as having a solid campaign platform.

I'm very appreciative of my experience during the elections. Even if I had lost, the knowledge and patience I gained during the campaign is something I will always carry with me.

Running for an elected position was truly one of the highlights of my college career. I believe the skills I learned while running for office and during my time as student body president will last a lifetime.

Contact: Tammy Schlinger
Address: 1204 5th Ave. NE, Mandan, ND 58554
Phone: (701) 663-3303

The First Woman SG President at Texas A&M University

By Brooke Leslie
1994-95 Student Government Association President
Texas A&M University

Introduction

Leslie, 25, served as Student Government Association president at Texas A&M, where she also was named Cotton Bowl Queen in 1993. In 1991, Leslie served as Texas FFA vice president and was a counselor for freshman orientation.

After graduating in 1995 with a degree in agricultural development, Leslie is attending law school at the University of Texas at Austin.

How Leslie Broke Through the Glass Ceiling at Texas A&M

It was a moment we had been waiting for a very long time. My campaign staff and I stood huddled together as name after name was read. When the Election Commissioner finally reached the last result of the night, I was quite sure that the hundreds of people gathered could hear my heart beating.

". . .and the 1994-95 student body president is...Brooke Leslie!"

From that moment on, it was all a blur of cheers, flash bulbs, and happy tears. We had done what many had called "the impossible." Texas A&M University had just elected its first female student body president — me. Unbelievable. Even though Texas A&M is the third-largest university in the nation with 43,000 students, A&M's roots are largely in its history as a highly conservative, all male, all military school. My election was more than a personal victory—it was a sign of the transformation of a time-honored institution.

So how did we do it? Work, work, organization, and more work. And most importantly, people on my team believed in me and my vision and that I was the best person for the job.

Decide why you want to run. When debating whether to run for president, I did a lot of soul searching. I had to be sure I was running for the right reason. It's very easy to get caught up in the "glamour" of elections and campaigns. I've seen past student leaders run for all the wrong reasons. Too many candidates just want to boost their egos, pack their resumes, and grab power. I wanted to give something back to A&M. Texas A&M gives so much to its students. There's a tremendous sense of family based on a unique sense of loyalty and school spirit.

Was I was ready to give one year of my life to Texas A&M. Was I really the best person for the job at the time? Would the school be a better place after my term of office?

My experience was on my side. I had served as speaker protempore of the student senate and was judicial board chair, so I had a working knowledge of the other two branches. My involvement in the College of Agriculture and many other campus groups contributed to my leadership experience and gave me a broad base of support on which to run.

After coming to the conclusion that I wanted to give back as much as my school had given to me, and with much support from my friends and family, I decided to give it a go. And that's when the real work began.

First, I chose a campaign manager. I needed someone whom I trusted as a close friend, but who also wasn't afraid to tell me when I was wrong. I chose the speaker of the Student Senate, Toby Boenig, a good friend since our high school FFA days. Toby and I started planning right away. We developed a timeline and research planks for our platform. We also considred who we needed on our campaign staff and which major constituencies were necessary to win.

From the beginning, this campaign was a team effort. We decided that the best way to build a staff was to target each of the major groups on campus. We recruited one very active student from each of A&M's 10 colleges, three big student organizations (Student Union, Student Government, and the Corps of Cadets), the Greek system, and the Residence Halls. We also appointed two students to be in charge of platform research, two to coordinate scheduling, and one who worked solely on strategy. These 23 students were our "core" staff.

Advance planning is critical. There is a formal campaign period, which is two and one-half weeks in March. But seven months before the election, we began meeting informally once a week. We were trailblazers in a sense — candidates had never planned so far ahead. We developed and employed a campaign strategy, where others had thrown things together at the last minute. Our preparation not only gave us a strong edge on the competition, but it narrowed the field. Several potential candidates probably were discouraged from running.

Usually there are six or seven candidates for president, but I had only one opponent. He had been class president for three years, was very active, and had great name recognition on campus. We was very well-liked and was a good friend to many, including me. He definitely had the edge going in. However, in the end, the difference was good planning, a dedicated campaign staff, and lots of hard work.

Months before the elections, Toby and I meticulously planned each meeting, setting an agenda and discussing goals to accomplish. My core staff members were very busy with their own activities, and I wanted to make the most of their time. Those first meetings were really general planning sessions. We discussed everything from campaign colors to platform ideas. At all times, the staff meetings operated much like a democracy. We often would vote on controversial decisions, and I always trusted in the group's gut feelings and opinions. As the candidate, I had final say, but we never had any major disagreements. My platform consisted of my ideas, but they were fully developed with the help of my volunteers.

At the beginning, we had to decide how to deal with the "woman issue." We decided not to use gender as part of our

After hearing the election results, Brooke Leslie celebrates her victory with friends and supporters, knowing that the hard work of fulfilling her platform promises lies ahead.

campaign strategy. Just as I wanted to run for only the right reasons, I wanted to be elected for only the right reasons as well. The important issues were my qualifications, my leadership credentials, and my vision— NOT which public restroom I used.

We were allowed a campaign budget of only $500, which doesn't go very far when you're trying to reach 43,000 voters. We obviously couldn't afford to buy newspaper, television, or radio ads. so we were forced to do things creatively and inexpensively. We passed out brochures at bus stops, and we had students standing with big signs on the corners of major intersections. (Since my election, the spending limits have been increased to about $1,500).

Three months before the election, meetings became more frequent as we began to assemble a larger staff. We hoped to have about 150 people working during election week. Their individual assignments would include shoe polishing hundreds of vehicles, knocking on 5,000 dorm room doors, and speaking to more than 700 student organizations. We tried to get someone from each student group to endorse us. A group of 150 volunteers easily could turn into a logistical nightmare. But we were ready with computer databases, an extensive filing system, and a very organized plan.

My opponent was involved in residence halls, and since the 10,000 students living on campus can be a formidable voting group, we hit them hard. All 5,000 dorm rooms were split into sections of 100, and two people were paired to go room-to-room in their assigned sections. Each pair had been coached and had practiced the art of door-to-door campaigning. Each person had a packet explaining everything they needed to know and how to encourage students to vote for me. They also were given presorted flyers, pamphlets, and "Brooke Leslie" paraphernalia.

Develop a flyer strategy. The flyer-crew members, numbering close to 50, each were in charge of one or two campus buildings during the two weeks of campaigning. Our goal was to cover every available wall space, door, and bulletin board within the first 30 minutes of the official campaigning period, which started at 12:01 a.m. Our flyers were the first ones to appear on literally thousands of bulletin boards around campus. Each flyer was checked daily to make sure it wasn't destroyed or covered over.

The speaker crew, numbering about 30, was responsible for attending meetings, dinners, and social functions — really any event that had more than two "Aggies" in attendance. I personally spoke at as many functions as my schedule would allow, but at prime meeting times, more than 35 meetings might be going on simultaneously. It was physically and logistically impossible to speak at more than 10 meetings each hour. I relied upon "speaker teams" made up of two volunteers who addressed groups about my campaign. All of the teams went through an orientation and practice session. These duos worked extraordinarily well for both speaking and door knocking. Most importantly, it was a positive experience for those involved with my campaign. It's imperative that you know and prepare your speakers. On such a big campus, there was no way I personally could meet every voter. My

EXPERIENCE	PLATFORM	PLATFORM
STUDENT GOVERNMENT	**STUDENT SERVICES**	**FINANCES**
-**Legislative Branch**-	-**Parking Garage**-Initiate construction of a new parking facility on campus in order to alleviate congestion caused by lack of space availibility.	-**Financial Aid**-Lobby Texas Legislature and Congress to increase funding for student financial aid, including Pell Grants, Hinson-Hazlewood Loans, and others.
Student Senate Speaker Pro-Tempore		
Internal Affairs Chair		
Off-Campus Senator		
Rules and Regulations Committee		
-**Judicial Branch**-	-**Camp Aggie**-Begin construction on a leadership retreat center in order that students may have a specific facility owned and operated by TAMU for use by all organizations, such as Fish Camp.	-**Scholarships**- Decrease GPA requirement for Excellence Award Scholarship in order to broaden accessability of funding to students contributing to the University through involvement in campus activities.
Judicial Board Chair		
University Disciplinary Appeals Panel		
-**Executive Branch**-		
Chancellor's Advisory Board-		
Vice Chair of Student Affairs	-**Book Swap**- Provide an avenue for which students will have easier access to buying books at a lower cost.	-**Student Service Fee Allocation**- Research possibilities of restructuring the Student Senate Finance Committee to allow for an equally fair process to ensure the best possible distribution of $6.8 million in Student Services Fees.
SGA Executive Council		
Presidential Search Advisory Committee		
Legislative Study Group		
President's Speakers Bureau		
ADDITIONAL INVOLVEMENT	**UNIVERSITY RELATIONS**	**ACADEMICS**
Fish Camp Counselor	-**External Media Relations**- Restructure Student Government's Public Information Office in order to publicize and improve perception of *all* aspects of Texas A&M to the world community.	-**Academic Counseling**-Establish consistent counseling policies throughout all colleges, as well as initiate a freshman "Plan Of Service" program, which includes mandating the contact of advisors before registration.
Camp Bryant		
Camp Poenisch		
Camp Busch		
Golden Key National Honor Society		
Class of '94 Council	-**Honor Code**-Preserve the Aggie Code of Honor as well as Texas A&M's high moral standard by initiating a campaign to establish a university wide policy that will hold students accountable for their actions.	-**Student Senate Legislation**-Work with University Administration to secure past legislation such as extra reading days and release of teacher evaluations.
Southwestern Black Student Leadership Conference-Hostess		
American Cancer Society Spokesperson		
1993 Cotton Bowl Representative		
COLLEGE OF AGRICULTURE	**DIVERSITY**	**CAMPUS SAFETY**
College of Agriculture Council	-**Cultural Sensitivity**- Support cultural enrichment education in order to increase awareness and respect for all Aggies and ensure Texas A&M University's world-class status.	-**Crimestoppers**-Work with author of Student Senate Legislation to implement program in order to decrease campus crime.
AgriSpeakers		
Collegiate FFA		-**Lighting**-Provide better lighting in remote parking areas such as Olson, Kleberg, and Zachry to ensure a safer campus.
Saddle and Sirloin		
Agricultural Communicators of Tomorrow		

Leslie's platform included specifics on how she would accomplish her goals after she won.

speaking crew had to represent me and leave a positive impression in the minds of potential voters.

In two and one-half weeks, I personally spoke to about 200 different groups, including 30 to 40 outfits in the Corps of Cadets, the ROTC program at A&M. I was there every day at 5:30 a.m. and could catch three or four outfits before they went on their morning run. Members of the Corps vote in very high percentages, but I didn't originally expect to get a majority of their support. Fortunately, I did gain the support of many of their leaders, which turned out to be a critical factor in my election.

The platform is your foundation. I was most proud of our platform. I was determined to promise the students of Texas A&M benefits that could be delivered. As mentioned before, our small core staff had two full-time students dedicated strictly to platform research. The entire group of 23 brainstormed, then I sat down with the "platformers" and narrowed down the issues. After researching, the three of us came up with a definite plan of action.

The issues we chose included offering scholarships based on leadership and service to our campus, building a new parking garage, building a leadership retreat center for student organizations, and starting a "campus crimestoppers" program. When it came time for the debates, the endorsement interviews with the media, the Q&A sessions at various organizations, and general campaigning, I believe we had the edge because we had more than ideas — we had a plan for execution. I believe the voters could see my committment to the issues. My opponent had some great ideas, but didn't offer specific solutions. My opponent would say, "We need more parking." I would say "Here's where a new parking garage should be, this is who will pay for it, and this date is when it will be done."

We had one well-attended debate. Five student leaders from different organizations get to ask questions of each of us, we answer, then the other is permitted to rebut. It's usually a packed house with 1,500 students.

My 13-point plan and well-researched platform were critical to getting the endorsement of our campus newspaper, *The Battalion*. The campus was frustrated with unfulfilled promises and passive government. My plan of action was exactly what *The Batallion* was looking for. I remember telling the editorial board in my three and one-half hour interview, "I want you to be a watchdog during my term—hold me to my promises." Not only were they a watchdog, but the paper proved to be a helpful ally during the election.

We were allowed to campaign up until midnight on the night before the elections. At midnight, after working nonstop for weeks, we said a prayer. I was at peace with myself, knowing we had done everything possible to win. Win or lose, we had fought the good fight. When the results were finally tabulated, I had earned about 61 percent of the roughly 14,000 votes cast.

The first commitment I made as student body president was to implement my platform. Achieving my campaign promises was to be our top priority and many hours of hard work went toward that goal. Eleven months later, our goal was reached and my committment to the students fulfuilled. The short-term projects were completed and the long-range items were fully planned, approved, and funded.

Campaigning is one of the most difficult times any person can go through. You will learn who your true friends are—quite an eye-opening experience. Politics and personalities affect every campaign, even a student election. Some people I called "friends" turned against me simply because they felt my opponent had a better chance of winning. I learned to have very thick skin. Inevitably, some people who you think are supporters are not. It's a hard thing to swallow.

Make school a priority. I didn't go to class for about a month and a half, but luckily my department was supportive and my professors were very understanding. Since I was planning on attending law school, grades still were important to me, so I tried hard to keep my GPA high. That semester, my GPA did drop, but only from a 3.70 to a 3.65.

Campaigning is a true test of willpower, strength, dedication, and belief in yourself and your school. But the process of running for student body president is also one of the most rewarding experiences you will have. An opportunity to give back to something in which one believes, such as your school, is a true blessing. Grab hold of that opportunity, no matter what anyone says. I'm glad that I did. I was blessed with the most amazing, fulfilling, hardest, best year of my life.

Contact: Brooke Leslie
Address: Route 2, Box 040, Glen Rose, TX 76043

The Incumbent Vice President Wins the Presidency at Texas Christian

By Sharon Selby
1996 TCU House of Student Representatives President
Texas Christian University

Introduction

Selby, 22, served as student body president at TCU, a private university with about 6,000 students, until January 1997. In addition to her presidential duties, Selby was involved in the Kappa Alpha Theta sorority and interned with the Tyson Organization political consulting group.

After graduating in May 1997 with degrees in political science and French, Selby will attend law school at New York University.

How Selby Learned From Previous Elections to Win

The night I decided to run for student body president, I immediately enlisted my roommate, close friend, and former vice presidential campaign manager to help out. Perhaps out of friendship or maybe some strange desire to undergo major stress, Susan Banzer agreed to have another go at the political process. Thus began the first planning session of the "Selby for President" campaign.

After serving as vice president for a year, I was hooked on student government. I think there's often a natural succession between the two positions and that the experience I gained as vice president paved the way for me to become president. We'd already run a successful hotly contested campuswide campaign once. Winning that election gave me confidence that I could win a presidential bid.

I had worked very closely with the previous president to learn the behind-the-scenes details. Once I started working on projects and policies, I wanted to continue to pursue our goals, as well as new ideas and needs we had discovered, such as computer networking and renovating the residence halls. We also wanted to expand TCU Vanguards, a new orientation program for freshmen. In light of these ongoing and new projects, I believed that it would help to have a president who had been in on the discussion already and wouldn't have to learn everything from scratch.

My platform consisted largely of promoting my previous SG experience. The main ideas were improving freshmen retention, increasing resources for transfer students, and getting a computer lab for the student center. I also stressed the need for improved communication between the student body and the House because students sometimes see the House as an elite group. We also wanted to develop more personal relationships among House members, so they would be more willing to work together, write joint bills, and to interact socially outside of the weekly meetings.

Learn from past presidents. Before you decide to run, it's wise to acquaint yourself with past administrations. This gives you a historical perspective of what has been tried, what has worked, and what has failed. This understanding of the feasibility of new projects proves immeasurably helpful once you're elected. I talked with former student body officers, including the treasurer from several years ago, and House advisors.

Being an "insider candidate" was an advantage, in my opinion, but it often can work against you. Sometimes there's a sense that the House needs to be revamped or that we need to get rid of all House leaders and start fresh. Some candidates are successful running as outsiders.

Having a detailed platform will go for naught if it's not communicated to students. A great advantage in having Susan as my campaign manager a second time was that she was well-aware of the election codes and the "do's and don't's" of elections. We thought about this a lot over the summer and then met in mid-September. We immediately made lists of the different ways we were going to campaign. I wasn't officially a candidate until the two-week filing period. Announcing intentions beforehand is considered "early campaigning," which isn't permitted.

At TCU, the spending limit for House campaigning is only $60. Runoff elections allow another $20 budget, and receipts in both elections must be turned in to prove that the limit isn't exceeded. TCU's spending limitations sometimes force campaigns to look somewhat amateurish, because you just can't spend much on anything. This forces all candidates to be more creative and less reliant on printed materials, banners, flyers, stickers, and other typical campaign promotional materials. Candidates have to emphasize public speaking and personal contact with potential voters.

With our $60 budget, we had enough to buy name badges for supporters and to make posters, flyers, and yard signs. We also had some "Selby for President" flags put on straws in the cafeterias. Other election rules include no campaigning off-campus (which means no advertising or publicity on cars, such as shoe polish on windows), restrictions on size and placement of all posters and signs, and a requirement to budget a "fair market value" for all donated items.

To keep costs down, we bought colored paper in reams from a discount paper store and then made copies ourselves at Office Depot, which saved over places with higher prices like Kinko's. This allowed us to buy name badges and give them only to those supporters we knew would wear them during the whole campaign. We passed out less expensive paper badges to everyone else.

We used color to get attention in both elections. Most candidates here stick with a consistent color scheme. My opponent in the runoff, for example, used orange. While using white paper is often much less expensive, signs and posters may get lost in the midst of all the other posters and flyers on campus. We chose the same shade of blue and fonts similar to those used in my vice presidential race, which we believe proved helpful.

Use a slogan to get attention. We also opted for the slogan "It's Time" on all our materials. In my previous race, we didn't think it was that important, but for the presidential bid, we wanted something to associate with my name. We wanted to stress that my previous experience had prepared me for the position and for the different or new issues that my platform raised. I used the slogan subtly in my speeches, such as "It's time to address the issue of technology..." We didn't want to appear too "slick," yet we gave a short, verbal association with the campaign to hopefully trigger a connection with the platform.

We put the signs all around campus. Campaign publicity on "The Mall" area is limited to 10 signs, and you can't have more than 10 signs in each residence hall or more than four in each academic building. We put yard signs at the parking lot entrances and exits and lined the main walkways. Candidates just plaster the walk from the cafeteria to the library, which is a major pedestrian thoroughfare.

Susan was great at rounding up volunteers, mainly from our sorority. Of the 130 sisters, almost all actively helped and all of them wore buttons. She also recruited friends among the resident assistants and targeted volunteers in each residence hall. When we sent out thank-you notes after the election, we had more than 200 volunteers who had contributed.

It's essential to give students tasks when they offer to help, otherwise they'll lose interest fast. Susan also formed teams for each component of the campaign. Small groups made the flyers, posters, stakes, etc. Over the last two successful campaigns, I've developed an organizational chart for members' responsibilities that I use when giving presentations about running for office and to give to potential candidates when they come by for advice.

Elections always are held on a Tuesday, then the runoffs, if necessary, are two days later on Thursday. We knew we would have a runoff since there were three strong candidates. With $20 more to spend, we covered the campus with flyers and signs saying "It's time to vote again Thursday." Our signs included the date, to publicize the election as well. While students might forget to vote, many others don't know there's an election.

We recruited a huge "campaign day" team to help work the actual polls, which are outside two main cafeterias. This is very

Selby's supporters wore creative shirts to promote her outside of the TCU Student Center.

important in that many students are influenced by who they see publicly supporting you and some will arrive at the polls still undecided.

Yet standing at the polls isn't enough — it takes a huge effort to get students to take the time to vote. We assigned teams to canvass residence halls on the days of the election and the runoff. We focused on freshmen dorms because first-year students vote more readily, as well as halls where we knew students would vote in blocks.

Make reminder calls to friends. Telephone calls on election day also were helpful. We only made local calls to students living on-campus or in Fort Worth, because long distance calls would have counted against our total budget. It was pretty informal — just friends reminding friends to vote. We opted to have volunteers call only students with whom they were personally acquainted. In the past, other candidates had left mechanized messages on students' answering machines, so we wanted to avoid any "annoying" backlash.

We also recruited students to send endorsement letters to

their friends. As one of 14 OSAs (Orientation Student Assistants) on campus, I met freshmen when they first arrived and helped them get acquainted with campus. Not only did I enjoy the job, but I got to know a great number of students. This position allowed me to write all of the students who had been in my orientation groups over the previous two summers.

I also had given all the "presidential welcomes" at each of seven orientation camps the summer before, since the House president was out of the country, which probably increased my exposure. Attending orientation is the first thing new students do when they get here, so many of them remembered me at election time.

Public speaking takes a tremendous amount of time and is crucial to every campaign. Two debates were staged, yet were poorly attended. Like most schools, it's hard to get the "average" student to really care, so you get a lot of newspaper and House people at the debates.

Don't worry about endorsements. Before elections, our student newspaper *The Skiff* does a "voter's guide" spread which includes each candidate's photo and responses to three questions. While *The Skiff* endorses candidates, I wasn't their choice. In hindsight, I think *The Skiff*'s endorsement may actually have a negative effect. There's a theory that it's a kiss of death, as there's something of an anti-*Skiff* sentiment on campus.

Most candidates made the usual rounds, speaking to fraternities and sororities and international, cultural, and professional groups, but we tried extremely hard to speak to every organization possible. In two weeks, I did about 60 speeches at student group meetings. I brought brochures to every speech, allowing me to keep my presentation short and succinct while offering detailed information on my experience and platform. I had volunteers help organize my schedule and set up appointments, but some groups agreed to let me "drop in," which created more flexibility and more exposure.

The actual race was interesting. Four candidates filed, including myself, the current student body secretary, the incumbent

Before serving as president, Selby won her race to become House of Representatives vice president, an election that taught her how to campaign successfully for a campuswide job.

Permanent Improvements Committee chairman, and a student with no previous House experience. Interestingly, all candidates were Greek, so the issue of independents vs. Greeks never came up in the race.

My sorority was a huge wealth of both moral and physical support. Members were with me at six in the morning to hang signs, sent many notes of encouragement, and wore "Selby" buttons throughout the entire campaign. In the runoff, we faced the P.I. chair, who was a member of a strong fraternity, so we were evenly matched as far as the number of campaign volunteers. About 33 percent of students at TCU is Greek, so we also concentrated on pulling in the vote of non-Greeks.

We led in the first election. The runoff was tough, and the result was close — a victory margin of 53 votes. I got 763 votes, while my opponent tallied 710. Voter turnout was higher than previous years, reaching almost 25 percent (or 1,500 of the 6,000 undergrads), mainly because of the competitive nature of the race and the fact that there were four qualified candidates.

Once the polls close at 7 p.m., most candidates usually head home to rest. We had some friends around, but we didn't have a big party. We were all so tired, so we just watched *ER* and waited. Everyone jumped each time the phone rang. Finally, we got the call announcing the results, but there wasn't a lot of time to celebrate or relax, as all candidates have to remove their campaign materials within 36 hours. This can be a little awkward when you see your opponents out taking down their flyers.

I'm amazed at how little sleep we got during the campaign. The late hours and constant speaking, smiling, and campaigning are draining, yet the challenge of an election and the experience you gain are invaluable. It's helpful to understand the logistics of running a campaign, to learn how to get people involved and invested in a challenge, and to realize that you can't do it on your own. I encourage students to run if they are remotely interested — weigh the odds, develop a strategy, and go for it. I believe the adage "You'll never know unless you try" says it all. Just remember that once you win, the real challenge begins!

Contact: Sharon Selby
Address: 1912 Ruth Drive, Garland, TX 75042
Phone: (972) 840-3536

Overcoming Negative Publicity To Win At Western Washington University

By Leslie Keller
1996-97 Associated Students President
Western Washington University

Introduction

In addition to her responsibilities as Associated Students president, Keller spends the rest of her time competing on the women's varsity golf team and studying for a degree in outdoor recreation.

After graduating in December 1997, Keller, 22, will attend graduate school to specialize in student affairs in higher education administration.

How Keller Battled Negativity to Win At Western

Getting involved as a freshman, setting goals, and being enthusiastic are three characteristics which undoubtedly helped me become Associated Students president.

Located in Bellingham, Washington, Western is a regional university with about 10,700 students. Most Western students focus on academics, so getting involved in extracurricular activities such as student government is rare. Those students who do take on the extras are excellent examples of student leaders; they balance classes, a social life, and a demanding job in student government.

I've been involved since my freshman year, but I couldn't have envisioned then that I would be A.S. president as a senior. My friends probably would disagree because they know I'm not the type of person to watch things happen. I have to be right in the middle of it.

As a first-year student, I got involved in Hall Council and the

Residence Hall Association (RHA). I became RHA president my sophomore year, was A.S. vice president for internal affairs as a junior, then decided that I wanted to run for A.S. president during my senior year.

Every April, we hold the Associated Students Board of Directors elections for president and six vice presidents. The spring 1996 contest — my election — was one of the most controversial Western students have ever witnessed.

Mine was one of only two contested races, while the other five positions were unopposed incumbents. I won with 71 percent of the vote, which may imply that my campaign was easy. But in reality, it was the longest and ugliest month of my life.

It was reminiscent of some national elections. First, there was a major change in the voting process, as well as the election and campaign dates. The grievance board was tainted by allegations of bias. And lastly, four of the six vice presidential candidates were incumbents, which everyone knew would discourage other students from running.

All of this contributed to one of the lowest voter turnouts Western has seen in a long time. Only 468 students voted (or about four percent), compared to 3,068 voters three years before.

On our campus, we try to keep Associated Students elections as simple as possible — $80 is each candidate's campaign spending limit, and we only allow two weeks of campaigning.

Our school newspapers, *The AS Review* (the student government PR paper) and *The Western Front* aren't allowed to endorse candidates, and neither are clubs and organizations. Clubs can't vote officially as blocks or force their members to vote or work for one candidate. Western also doesn't have a Greek system, so that wasn't a factor like it is on other campuses. You must be able to "sell" yourself to individual students, not power groups.

Since I had been involved in A.S. for three years prior to my race for president, I had seen many good and bad campaigns — I knew the ropes and had the support to get elected. I looked to friends, fellow candidates, university faculty and staff, and past A.S. board members for help with everything from posting flyers and writing speeches to supporting me during the frustrating grievance battles.

Through these contacts, I was able to speak at hall councils, classes, and RHA and elections forums. We also were allowed to set up tables in the coffee shop, a major campus thoroughfare, and distribute campaign literature. We don't have debates, mainly because the forums in the past have been so poorly attended, but we're considering them in the future.

Know your stuff when you speak. In addressing student groups, I made a positive impression, because I knew my audience, had self confidence, and was prepared and knowledgeable. I'm also, thankfully, a people person and don't mind speaking in public either. I presented myself as the typical Western student and was visible on campus speaking at forums, talking with students in the dining halls, or chatting in the campus square. I often stayed after meetings to talk with students. I was accessible and approachable, and I feel like I shared my ideas in a non-pushy way.

My platform focused on offering child care, which is a statewide issue, forming a student senate, publishing faculty evaluations on our web page, improving communications between the administration and students, improving the efficiency of our student technology fee process, and increasing A.S.'s visibility.

My final issue was that I was the candidate who had the experience. I told voters that I would finish projects that I had started. So often student government leaders take on tasks, then never finish because they graduate and move on after their term of office. I vowed that I would stay on another year after my presidency to finish our projects.

As far as publicity, we used banners and posters heavily. Each candidate is allowed six banners and one flyer per "post" outside most buildings. We're permitted to hand out as many flyers to individuals as we want, but we do have to pick up the trash afterward since our campus is heavily into recycling.

Be ready for reporters' questions. We also wrote articles for *The Western Front* and the election version of the SG paper. I planned ahead for interviews with reporters and tried to give thoughtful and concise responses to their questions. Being prepared helped me create a positive image in the paper, although this often can be out of a candidate's control. Luckily, most of the press I got was positive, although it was frustrating to see the headline "Keller Wins A.S. Presidency In Tainted Election" in *The Western Front* after our victory. It's not the kind of headline you want to send home to your parents and friends.

On the other hand, my opponent had not been involved in A.S. previously and wasn't knowledgeable about the issues. He rarely showed up to speaking engagements. He might have been intimidated by the fact that I was so well known on campus.

Once the race really got rolling, just like many national elections, problems started cropping up. **Avoid mud slinging at all costs.** First, negative campaigning reared its ugly head. One of my friends, without my knowledge, defaced some of my opponent's flyers, was caught, and was charged with a grievance. While I wasn't personally involved, it still made me look bad to have a supporter breaking the rules.

I also had a total of three grievances filed against me before the election, then had to wait for the verdicts, which was demoralizing. The grievance board could have given any penalty it wished, from forcing me to quit campaigning to making me take down all of our posters. For example, my opponent was prohibited from campaigning at one part of campus when he was found guilty of "door knocking" in residence halls, which is against election rules.

One of the grievances was about the new voting process. Because of the schools' recent growth, many students had suggested that there should be multiple polling places. In the past, there had been only one and it wasn't computerized. The seven A.S. board members came up with an excellent idea to scan university ID cards at the polls to prevent students from voting more than once, but the plan couldn't be implemented in time.

So we came up with an alternative way to encourage students to vote. We mailed each student a yellow voter "registration" postcard, which they were supposed to bring to the polls on election day. At the time, we thought this would ensure that students only got one vote.

In hindsight, it was a major mistake. We quickly learned the hard way that the postcard plan was ineffective. Students just don't read "junk" mail and they don't remember dates. The result was a very low voter turnout and an increase in the number of absentee voters. Instead of only a handful like in the past, there were 175 absentee ballots cast this year.

At the time, I was serving as a board member and was partially responsible for planning this new election process. My involvement became another huge controversy, mainly because absentee ballots are collected only five feet from my office door. In the past, if you were going to be gone on election day, you picked up a ballot at the A.S. Board office, then mailed it in. This year, any stu-

Keller's volunteers hang a campaign banner outside Frasier Hall, near the center of campus.

dent who "lost" the postcard was allowed to vote absentee on election day. I say lost because I believe a lot of students got the cards, but discarded them, then said they never got them.

Obviously, some of my opponents were convinced that I could sway voters since my office was so close to the polls, so they filed another grievance. Despite the fact that I had spent most of the day locked in my office or canvassing campus, the grievance board voted to void all of the absentee ballots.

After the elections, we made a rule to prevent A.S. Board members from being involved with any future elections. I know now that elections shouldn't be organized by possible candidates. It's obviously a major conflict of interest.

The worst part is that I knew all of this at the time and tried to shift my responsibilities to others (I was the supervisor of the election coordinator and was supposed to be the chair of the grievance board), but it was too late.

The bottom line is that despite all of my good intentions, I was caught in the middle of a mess, and my political destiny at Western was left in the hands of five peers on the grievance board. I believe I shed more tears during my two weeks of campaigning than I have in my life.

Having to wait for the verdicts really can dampen the spirits of a campaign and to make it even worse, I had to be out of town with the golf team, which meant I had to get the results by phone. Dealing with these controversies also made it more difficult to campaign because I was both an A.S. presidential candidate and an A.S. Board member who helped design the election process.

Thankfully, despite some bad press in *The Western Front*, our campus newspaper, my supporters still were behind me, because they knew who I was and what I was about. And later, I was cleared of all the charges.

Right after the elections, however, the election coordinator and a previous A.S. board member formed a new club to watch over the new officers. Their primary mission was to recall three of the newly elected members, including me. I still don't understand completely why they wanted us removed from office, but I think it was petty. They personally disliked us and were trying to get even. It seemed pretty immature. They tried to circulate a petition demanding a recall, but it was unsuccessful.

It's sad, because I still believe the election coordinator had the potential to be the best in school history. She was very familiar with A.S., had run for office herself, and had great ideas. I think she got overwhelmed by the changes, grievances, and the pressure. Things got personal as a result.

Learn from your struggles. All of these issues made me miserable at the time, but as I look back, I now realize that I learned many things, such as how to deal with people who didn't support me as a candidate, how to stand up for myself during tough circumstances, and that some people deal with their frustrations differently, sometimes resorting to petty pay-back tactics. If I ever run for office in the future, I'll be ready for dirty-pool politics.

Overall, these incidents didn't really damage my campaign, but they did impact my personal and emotional well being. I learned from this experience that you need to be strong to pursue an elected position. Everyone is watching and talking about you, both positively and negatively. You just need to believe in yourself, hold your head high, and keep a positive attitude.

I have always taken my involvement in student government seriously. I also enjoy what I do, or I wouldn't be doing it. The people I've met and the leadership skills I've developed are just as valuable as my classes and my major. In fact, a lot of what I do in A.S. has given me hands-on experience in what I'll be doing later in my career in student affairs.

Despite all of the struggles I had and battles I fought, I don't regret getting involved or running for office. The experience I've gained is immeasurable.

Whether you win or lose — and I have lost my fair share of elections, including three years in a row throughout high school — the experience makes you stronger. I encourage all students who are interested in politics or in helping people to get involved in student government.

Contact: Leslie Keller
Address: 1975 S. 368th Place,
Federal Way, WA 98003
Phone: (360) 650-3460 or (360) 733-7632
Fax: (360) 650-6507
E-Mail: n9344120@cc.wwu.edu or aspres@cc.wwu.edu

About the Editor

Butch Oxendine, 34, is president of Oxendine Publishing, Inc., the award-winning company that has published student magazines across Florida and the nation for more than 14 years. In 1993, Mr. Oxendine was named one of the top 100 entrepreneurs in the nation under the age of 30. In 1996, Oxendine Publishing was honored as one of the 100 fastest-growing private companies in Florida.

Mr. Oxendine has been published in more than 100 newspapers and magazines, and has been quoted or interviewed in more than 250 newspapers and magazines. He is a frequent speaker on leadership and student issues, including campus elections strategies, at conferences across the country.

Mr. Oxendine is president of the Pamela Helen Scott Memorial Scholarship, and is founding sponsor of the 11th annual Florida College Student of the Year awards program.

He has been named to Outstanding Young Men of America, Who's Who Among Young American Professionals, Who's Who in Emerging Leaders in America, Who's Who in U.S. Executives, Who's Who in American Advertising, Who's Who in the Southeast, and Who's Who of Global Business Leaders. He was named outstanding alumnus of Lake City Community College in 1995 and was nominated for Florida Community College Alumnus of the Year in 1993 and 1996.

Mr. Oxendine is a 1981 graduate of Suwannee High School in Live Oak, a 1983 honors grad of Lake City C.C., and attended the University of Florida. He is married to Kathryn Platt Oxendine and is the father of Leah Kathryn.

About Oxendine Publishing

For more than 14 years, Oxendine Publishing has produced magazines exclusively for college and high school students.

Nationally, Oxendine publishes the leadership-development magazine *Student Leader*, well-read by top campus leaders at nearly 900 colleges and universities. In Florida, Oxendine publishes the college magazines *Florida Leader* and *Careers & Majors*, as well as a version of *Florida Leader* for high school students.

Totalled, Oxendine's student-oriented magazines are read by hundreds of thousands of students at nearly 1,500 colleges and high schools nationwide.

The Gainesville, Florida-based company also is founding sponsor of the annual Florida College Student of the Year Award, a prestigious scholarship program that recognizes Florida's top campus achievers and leaders.

Oxendine plans to publish several other books for campus leaders, including:

OTHER BOOKS AVAILABLE NOW
✓ *Poster Secrets: How & Where To Hang Flyers On Your Campus*

COMING SOON
✓ *101 Money-Saving Ideas for Student Groups*
✓ *How To Start Your Own Campus Publication*
✓ *50 Fundraising Ideas That Really Work*
✓ *How To Get Along With Your Campus Media*
✓ *101 Ways to Motivate & Reward Your Staff*

FIND OUT WHY 900 COLLEGES LOVE STUDENT LEADER!

Subscribe to Student Leader, the Leadership Magazine Written Exclusively for Campus Activists!

S *tudent Leader* is perfect for Student Government members, Greek leaders, RAs, orientation leaders, officers and key members of other campus organizations, and other activists who want to improve their leadership, management, and communication skills!

EACH MAGAZINE FEATURES USEFUL ARTICLES:

- ■ National Student Government Salary Survey
- ■ How to get publicity and deal with the media
- ■ How to combat apathy and frustration
- ■ How to get student involved in community service
- ■ Fund-raising tips that actually work!

NEW BOOK · NEW BOOK · NEW BOOK

How To Use Campus Bulletin Boards For Effective PR & Recruiting

Postering Secrets:
How & Where to Hang Flyers On Your Campus

By the Editors of *Student* **LEADER**
The Magazine for America's Most Outstanding Students

New and proven ideas on how to design and distribute flyers to recruit new members and publicize your organization's fund raisers, meetings, and events. This 64-page workbook tells you exactly when, where, and how to display your posters and flyers around campus to get the best (and cheapest) exposure possible.

---------- **ORDER FORM** ----------

Order Yours Today!

❑My check is enclosed.
❑My purchase order is enclosed.
(Our federal tax ID#: 59-2821054)

❑Please send me _____ copies of *Poster Secrets: How & Where to Hang Flyers On Your Campus* at $11.95 each. (Get 5 or more for only $9.95 ea.)

Merchandise Total	$ _____
Shipping & handling @ ($1.50 per book)	$ _____
TOTAL:	$ _____

MAIL THIS PORTION WITH CHECK OR PURCHASE ORDER TO:
Oxendine Publishing, Inc., P.O. Box 14081, Gainesville, FL 32604-2081

Your Name/Title _____

School / Company / Organization _____

Address _____

City/State/Zip _____

Phone ( ) _____

■ **FAX** YOUR ORDER to: (352) 373-8120 ■ **CALL** (352) 373-6907
■ **SEND E-MAIL** to: oxendine@compuserve.com ■ **WEB:** http://www.studentleader.com